MOVING FROM SHAME
TO SELF-WORTH

MOVING FROM SHAME TO SELF-WORTH

Preaching and Pastoral Care

EDWARD P. WIMBERLY, Ph.D.

Abingdon Press
Nashville

MOVING FROM SHAME TO SELF-WORTH:
Preaching and Pastoral Care

Library of Congress Cataloging-in-Publication Data

Wimberly, Edward P., 1943–
    Moving from shame to self-worth: preaching and pastoral care/
Edward P. Wimberly.
        p.   cm.
    Includes bibliographical references.
    ISBN 0-687-08226-9 (alk. paper)
    1. Shame—Religious aspects—Christianity.   2. Shame in the Bible.
3. Jesus Christ—Teachings.   4. Preaching.   5. Pastoral counseling.
I. Title.
BT714.W55   1999
253.5'2—dc21   98-36535
                                                                                CIP

Unless otherwise noted, Scripture quotations are from the King James Version Bible

Scripture quotations noted RSV are from the Revised Standard Version of the Bible, copyright 1946, 1952, 1971 by the Division of Christian Education of the National Council of
the Churches of Christ in the USA. Used by permission.

Scripture quotations noted NRSV are from the New Revised Standard Version Bible.
Copyright © 1989 by the Division of Christian Education of the National Council of the
Churches of Christ in the USA. Used by permission.

Printed on acid-free, recycled paper.

00 01 02 03 04 05 06 07 08 — 10 9 8 7 6 5 4 3 2

MANUFACTURED IN THE UNITED STATES OF AMERICA

CONTENTS

FOREWORD

The Christian community is blessed with many brilliant contributions from tremendously gifted contemporary writers. The shelves of Christendom are stacked with invaluable resources that speak with resounding relevance to our modern church. Occasionally, one discovers a literary work of art that speaks to the depths of his or her soul. Dr. Edward Wimberly's publication, *Moving from Shame to Self-Worth: Preaching and Pastoral Care*, does just that for me.

In an age when schism and turfism are the prevailing order of the day, it is refreshing to discover one who possesses the character and competence to synergize two major disciplines to transform the lives of human beings. Dr. Wimberly reminds us that pastoral counseling has always been thought of as attending to the relational and personal needs of people through dialogue in one-to-one and interpersonal relationships. Preaching has always been thought of as communicating the gospel in a public community in a monologue style. Pastoral counseling embraces a more nonjudgmental and accepting attitude while preaching embraces a more moral perspective in which people are challenged to change their attitudes. The genius of this book is that the author brilliantly utilizes the art of storytelling to bridge the gap and illustrate the interdependence between these two essential disciplines for ministry. Pastors, pastoral counselors, and religious workers who worship or counsel will be equipped to engage the world after reading this most essential publication.

The halls of the academy and the corridors of the cathedral are reverberating with debate concerning the relevancy of the Holy Scriptures for the present age and the age to come. The foundation of this book is the relevancy of Scripture, especially stories that enhance our faith through the gospel of Jesus Christ. Specific experiences in the life and ministry of Jesus are explored to illustrate how Jesus engages the world to transform a shame-based and hierarchical culture into a shame-less and egalitarian community in which one experiences value as a child of God.

Students and practitioners in the academy and the cathedral will be well equipped to engage our complex and diverse culture as a result of this wonderful book. The Christian community is tremendously indebted to Dr. Edward Wimberly for sharing his views, and ultimately himself, to further the cause of Christianity.

As a former student, I am honored by this opportunity to share in a small way in such an enduring work of my mentor, Dr. Wimberly. I eagerly accept the challenge to begin moving from shame to self-worth.

McCallister Hollins
Senior Pastor
Ben Hill United Methodist Church
Atlanta, Georgia

ACKNOWLEDGMENTS

This book emerged out of a class at the Interdenominational Theological Center entitled Foundations for Ministry. The course began as a team taught course led by Calvin Morris, Brenda Wallace, and myself. At the beginning of the course, the focus was on the current Jesus debate that is gripping the public. As part of the course, a faculty colleague, Wayne Merritt, was invited to survey the latest literature on the current popular Jesus debate. From this review, I was able to visualize the convergence of the honor and shame value system of first-century Mediterranean culture and contemporary shame theory in psychology. When I saw the theoretical correspondence, I decided to write a book that would draw on the contemporary theories of shame and the scholarship of the Jesus debate and show how it is possible to construct stories that can be told in either preaching or pastoral counseling. I am truly indebted to my faculty colleagues and students from the Foundations for Ministry class who were part of the original vision for writing this book.

I am also appreciative of those dialogue partners who read the manuscript to assure that it does what I set out to accomplish. These people include McCallister Hollins, Cynthia Vaughan, Wallace Hartsfield, Dave Rensberger, Wayne Merritt, Maisha Handy, Margaret Wimberly, Tamara Battice, James H. Salley, Eben K. Nhiwatiwa, Michael McQueen, Pamela Jones, Joyce Guillory, and Lavern Windom. Great appreciation is also extended to the Interdenominational Theological Center and to my editors at Abingdon Press, who made sure I had the necessary resources and encouragement to complete this writing project.

INTRODUCTION

I recently conducted a church seminar entitled "Shame and Forgiveness," emphasizing Romans 8:26:

> Likewise the Spirit also helpeth our infirmities: for we know not what we should pray for as we ought: but the Spirit itself maketh intercession for us with groanings which cannot be uttered.

I defined shame as feeling unlovable, that one's life has a basic flaw in it. I tried to describe how we live in a shame-prone society in which fulfillment of our need to feel loved and cared for is rapidly disappearing; we begin to settle for any kind of relationship just to feel loved. The cure for shame, I insisted, is finding relationships with significant others in which we experience some semblance of nurture and care without having to turn ourselves inside out, in ways that only increase our shame, in order to meet other people's expectations. I emphasized that the Spirit of God works on our behalf to help us view ourselves as worthwhile; God also tries to lead us toward the kinds of relationships that help us see ourselves as valuable.

I emphasized, to the surprise of many, that, because we are human beings, forgiveness is not something within our power, and I concluded that forgiveness is a gift of the Spirit that comes as God leads us through the forgiving process. To forgive prematurely, I emphasized, could lead us back into relationships that increase our shame and feelings of self-degradation. The Spirit pushes us to forgive in ways that lead to our self-enhancement rather than our self-negation. In my lecture, I told many stories attempting to tap into the experiences of people, so that when the time came for altar prayer, people would be prepared to pray the prayer of discernment—a prayer asking God to reveal where God is at work in our lives, bringing healing to shame and our emotional wounds.

After praying at the altar, one woman stood up to give her testimony. That night she seemed to have reached a point at which she was ready to talk about what God had been doing in her life during the last two years. She began by saying that she was not what she presented herself to be at church. She had presented herself as a well-put-together person, who knew who she was and who had many positive things going on in her life.

All her effort to make herself seem acceptable was a facade, she said. Beneath this facade was a great deal of shame and low self-esteem. As a child, she had been molested. She explained that this molestation caused her to see herself in less than positive terms. Believing she was the dumping ground for other people's junk, she allowed people to discard their unwanted stuff on her until she reached midlife. She had been married several times, and each marriage had ended in divorce. As a result of her feelings of shame, she settled for nothing but sexual relationships with men.

After this long introduction to her early life, she said a change had come to her life over the last two years. God began to work within her from the inside out. God made her aware of how destructive her beliefs about herself were and how she was perpetuating her low self-esteem by the kinds of relationships she was establishing. She felt convicted about the destructive way she was living, particularly settling for sexual relationships and demanding nothing more from the men in her life. As a result of what she felt God was doing in her life, she became celibate in her relationships with men. After being obedient to the Spirit at work in her, she began to develop healthier relationships and began to feel good about herself.

The woman closed her testimony by saying that she needed to share what God had done in her life so she could set the record straight. She wanted others to know that things in her life were not always what they appeared to be.

The key to her testimony was the phrase, "I believe I have learned to feel about myself the way Jesus felt about himself." She meant that Jesus had a very positive attitude about himself, and she was developing the same mind about herself. She took literally the biblical admonition "Let this mind be in you, which was also in Christ Jesus" (Phil. 2:5).

This testimony reminded me of how important storytelling is to our growth and development. We learn about our faith and what can be possible for us in our spiritual lives from hearing what others have to say about what God is doing. A tradition in which I grew up sensitized me to the need to listen to and tell stories as a major dimension of spirituality. Hearing what others say helps us see some of the possibilities that exist for us.

My life has been shaped not only by a rich storytelling environment but also by bountiful stories of Jesus. Like the woman who gave the testimony, I also thought that what our world needs today is to mimic how Jesus felt about himself as a way to come to grips with our shame-oriented culture. Therefore, I set out to explore in-depth how Jesus felt about himself, his relationships with others, and his ministry. My hope is that we might emulate how Jesus felt about himself and that this can motivate us to move toward some of our God-given possibilities.

This book focuses on the convictions and beliefs that Jesus had about himself, about others, and about God's rule and reign as seen in his sayings and stories. For Christians, Jesus' sayings are evidence of the level of his emotional and mental health. Jesus was not a fanatical figure possessed with self-importance or with what others thought of him. Rather, he was a man whose primary vocation was to fulfill the mission that he believed he had in life. No matter what he faced in life he kept his mission and purpose in mind, and I contend that it was this mission and purpose that helped Jesus feel very positive about himself and his ministry.

Obviously the early church believed that it was possible to know the mind of Jesus and to shape its own orientation to life based on him. In this book, I take seriously the instructions of the early church. We contemporary Christians can learn a lot by trying to emulate the mind of Christ Jesus.

Philippians 2:5-8 recommends that those who read this passage mimic Jesus' incarnation. That is, we are to place love at the center of our lives the way Jesus did. We are to take on the mind of a disciple. I believe that Jesus' self-understanding as a servant of God put on earth to follow a particular mission should also be our self-understanding. From this self-understanding, our positive emotional, mental, and spiritual health flows. That is, wholeness and spiritual, emotional, mental, and interpersonal well-being are derived from our understanding of why God put us here on earth.

Jesus' convictions about himself, his relationships with others, and his ministry can show us how we need to believe about ourselves and act toward others. To this end, I will look at selected sayings and stories of and about Jesus and try to determine what Jesus said about his life and ministry. Attending to what Jesus said and exploring what he believed about himself, others, and his ministry, we can also learn what it means to take on the mind of Christ.

Once we have a handle on how Jesus felt, we can then move on to draw implications for our own lives. The major concern that I have is to address the crises of purpose and shame that are engulfing our society. These crises are evident in our addictive culture, a culture that reflects a lack of meaning and purpose. In addressing this concern, I will choose narrative, or storytelling, which is found so often in scripture, as a rhetorical style.[1] My concern is to develop stories that can be used in both preaching and pastoral counseling.

Storytelling is not normally associated with pastoral counseling, yet for more than a decade telling stories and using metaphors in counseling have been on the rise. These stories help us learn from Jesus how to feel about ourselves, our relationships, and our ministry. The hope is that we will be able to address the malady of lack of purpose and meaning in life.

THE METHOD OF STORYTELLING

Once the authentic sayings of Jesus have been identified, the next step will be to build stories based on Jesus' convictions and beliefs that can be told in preaching and in counseling. The stories will be constructed based on what Michael E. Williams calls *midrash,* whereby biblical stories are retold or contemporary stories constructed to reflect the values and beliefs that Jesus espouses.[2] I have also been influenced by Renita Weems, who retells biblical stories taking into consideration voices that have been previously silent.[3]

In addition to retelling the "old, old stories" and reconstructing new stories, it is important to identify what the stories are intended to do in preaching and in pastoral counseling. Today, reality is often thought of as being created or constructed primarily by the language we use and by the stories we hear.[4] Each person and community has an orientation to reality that is deeply ingrained. This is true for people in congregations and for people who come to pastoral counseling. Consequently, the beliefs and convictions that inform people's behavior, attitudes, feelings, and relationships are fairly well formed and must be addressed at some level if any significant changes are to take place in their lives.

Biblically, changing the already formed view of reality that people bring to events and relationships is done primarily through storytelling. Storytelling's function is to help shape the view of reality that influences us.[5] However, if stories shape us and form the convictions and beliefs we have of reality, changing these views must also be something that needs to be addressed. The function of challenging existing views of reality and replacing them is the work of parable, according to John Dominic Crossan. According to him the art of the parable is to undermine the hearer's structure of expectation so that the deep structures that underlie the hearer's view of the world are changed.[6] Parabolic stories are told in such a way that the person's view of the world is undermined and he or she is ready to accept another way of looking at things.

Crossan's view of story and parable is part of a literary-critical tradition. This tradition has some close parallels with the use of stories and metaphors in pastoral counseling. The metaphoric protocol is established to do the very same function as the parable.[7]

Building on these two distinct traditions of parable and metaphor, I suggest that there is a convergence of pastoral counseling and preaching. This convergence recognizes that reality and the ways of knowing reality are storied, and changing one's view of reality requires attending to people's stories. Moreover, preaching and pastoral counseling are arenas where stories are told that change people's view of reality. Consequently, this book takes seriously the two different settings in which stories are told and intends to design stories that have a transforming effect on people's lives.

This book is addressed to preachers and pastoral counselors who are interested in constructing stories that speak to people's emotional, spiritual, interpersonal, marital, and family needs. It is not enough to develop a theory of how preaching and pastoral counseling are related. It is important to present a method of developing stories that can be used in either pastoral counseling or preaching in order to accomplish specific purposes for those who hear sermons or who are in counseling relationships.

My basic thesis is that people in congregational pews and people who come to counseling often have similar problems and needs. Historically, preaching has attempted to bring a perspective to human problems, a perspective that is grounded in a faith tradition, while counseling has sought to plumb the depths of a person's resources and relationships to find a cure for emotional, spiritual, and interpersonal problems. However, with the emergence of constructive theory and a hermenuetical understanding of the meaning-making process, there is some overlap of the functions of preaching and counseling. Though the settings are different, both preaching and pastoral counseling function to help people bring meaning to their experience. Storytelling in both settings is viewed as a hermeneutical approach that assists in the meaning-making process.

Another overlap of pastoral counseling and congregational preaching is that each focuses on issues that clearly deal with meaning-making concerns that are personal, emotional, spiritual, and interpersonal in nature. Of even greater significance is the exploration of key personal issues in Jesus' life, which we as his followers can envisage as possible solutions to our dilemmas.

The personal issues that I would like to explore are those related to self-beliefs and self-convictions. What we believe about ourselves shapes our behavior toward ourselves, others, and God. Normally, what we believe about ourselves forms either positive or negative images, which we then act out in our lives. These images either nourish our growth and development or they contribute to our demise when they negatively affect our feelings about ourselves. Editing the negative images or pejorative life-forming narratives is the function and task of storytelling that I will explore.[8]

The world we live in today is fractured and less controlled by a cohesive worldview. In fact, there are many competing worldviews that we must choose from in order to bring meaning to our lives. These worldviews, or assumptive worlds, do not always help our self-esteem or self-affirmation. These assumptive worlds often produce a culture of shame that undermines our sense of self and works against our growth and positive mental, emotional, and spiritual health. The culture of shame to which this book speaks is characterized by a pervasive sense of worthlessness, being unlovable, and a feeling that there is a fundamental flaw in one's being.[9] Such feelings of shame come from a variety of sources, including increased evil and insensitivity toward other human beings (despite human progress), dehumanizing stereotypes that degrade physical and gender differences, child abuse, eating disorders, drug addiction, poverty, sexism, homophobia, classism, and racism. In addition, shame accompanies and is reflected in the breakdown of nuclear and extended families, consumer individualism, anomie, and isolation.[10] With this increase in shame comes an increase in violence, which some understand as the effort to break the oppressive internal and external shackles one feels.[11] Preaching and pastoral counseling take place in a world with divergent worldviews, where traditional relationships cannot be taken for granted. Shame is all too often the dominant experience of the self. Preaching and pastoral counseling must address this contemporary experience.

People in congregations and in pastoral counseling bring well-formed personal narratives fashioned and shaped by their experiences of shame. These personal narratives are what Merle R. Jordan calls *secular scriptures* in the sense that they have taken the place of the ancient scriptures in determining how one believes, thinks, and acts.[12] These secular scriptures become idols around which people have organized their lives and interpreted reality. Changing them requires divine and human intervention. Mere storytelling will not address these personal narratives that are rooted in secular scriptures. Pastoral counseling alone cannot address these scriptures. What is needed is a holistic approach involving preaching, pastoral counseling, and participation in church life that has some potential to change the shame-based narratives that undergird people's lives.

Given the staying power of secular scriptures, the parabolic dimension of stories, which challenges existing stories and personal narratives, must be an essential dimension of preaching and pastoral counseling. It is not enough to tell Bible stories or contemporary stories. Rather, stories, both biblical and contemporary, must be told that have as their goal disabling the secular scriptures so that a new and better world can be disclosed. This will take time and effort. This book is designed to help preachers and pastoral counselors attend to the shame-based secular scriptures that undergird people's lives.

PASTORAL THEOLOGY

I do not like the compartmentalized way in which preaching and pastoral counseling are separated in our thinking. Indeed, preaching and pastoral counseling are different dimensions and perspectives in practical ministry. However, from a pastoral and theological perspective, communicating the gospel and caring are intricately related. More precisely, they both aim at undermining the negative stories that hinder people from the wholeness that is promised by the gospel. Preaching, on the one hand, does this by focusing on the historical faith and proclaiming it through the sermon and through teaching. Pastoral counseling, on the other hand, does it through developing depth relationships using psychology and counseling. Therefore, the setting for addressing the negative narratives shaping the lives of people is different, but the use of parabolic stories is possible in both settings. It is through the use of parabolic stories that undermine the assumptive world of people for the purposes of disclosing a saving gospel that preaching and pastoral counseling are related. In short, the most important pastoral and theological feature of this book is the fact that it is possible to visualize ministry as holistic rather than compartmentalized.

METHOD OF DEVELOPING THE BOOK

The steps that I will follow in constructing stories are:

1. Focus on the words of Jesus as they appear in specific events of his ministry.
2. Determine whether the words Jesus used dealt with convictions and beliefs he held about himself, his relationships, or his ministry.
3. Determine the mimetic lesson that can be the focus of the design of a parabolic contemporary story.
4. Explore the contemporary shame problems or issues that are analogous to the issues and concerns that Jesus was addressing.
5. Form the parabolic story, drawing on the structural patterns of parables and protocols.
6. Show how the story can be used in a sermon and pastoral counseling.

I have divided my argument into three parts. Part 1 explores how Jesus came to grips with the shame and humiliation he faced in his own life and how we can imitate his manner of handling shame. Part 2 focuses on how Jesus dealt with the shame that others brought to him and the implications this has for how we can overcome shame by internalizing and reenacting Jesus' stories in our lives. Finally, Part 3 explores the parables of Jesus and their implications for helping us live lives based on nonshame-based values.

PART ONE

JESUS' HANDLING OF HIS OWN SHAME

It is often difficult to imagine that Jesus had to deal with issues related to shame. His life, however, was characterized by issues of shame related to the circumstances of his birth, his growth and development in his hometown, and his later ministry. Part 1 explores how Jesus came to grips with the shame that he confronted in his life and ministry.

CHAPTER ONE

BEYOND THE WORLD
OF SHAME

New research on the historical Jesus helps us to see that Jesus not only saw himself primarily as a person who was inaugurating a new world called the kingdom of God, he also saw himself as a participant in this new world to which he was inviting people. This new world was fundamentally different from the shame-based cultures that made up a world where only a few are privileged and deemed worthy. Thus, in Jesus' mind, there were two worlds, the world to come and the present world. The world to come was present but not completed, and it was based on an inclusive ethic rather than an exclusive one. This was demonstrated primarily by Jesus' healing ministry and his eating habits, both of which were attempts to bring about a shared egalitarianism.[1]

In this chapter I will begin to build stories, which can be used in preaching and pastoral counseling, centered on insights generated from reflecting on how Jesus felt about himself as a participant in a world that was egalitarian and nonshame-based. The specific focus of this chapter is on the temptations of Jesus. Guiding the development of this chapter will be (1) determining what Jesus believed about himself, (2) deriving the mimetic lesson to be learned, (3) examining the contemporary issues that this belief raises, and (4) constructing biblical and contemporary stories.

JESUS AS AN EGALITARIAN

Jesus' wilderness experience found in Luke 4:1-13, Matthew 4:1-11, and Mark 1:12-13 is described by Marcus J. Borg as follows:

Matthew and Luke agree that he spent a forty-day solitude in the wilderness, where he was tested by the lord of the evil spirits and nourished by beneficent spirits. They add that Jesus fasted and had a series of three closely related visions. In the first, Jesus was tempted by Satan to use his powers to change stones into bread. In the second and third, Jesus and Satan traveled together in the spirit world. The devil took Jesus to the highest point of the temple in Jerusalem, and then "took him up and showed him all the kingdoms of the world in a moment of time." Throughout, Satan tempted Jesus to use his charismatic powers in self-serving ways and to give his allegiance to him in exchange for all the kingdoms of the world.[2]

The fact that Jesus' public ministry was preceded by temptation is very important. It gives us a glimpse of the power of Jesus over Satan through the Spirit. Moreover, Jesus' dealing with Satan and his influence was very consistent with an overall theology of vanquishing Satan.[3] In short, the temptations of Jesus deserve attention when trying to ascertain how Jesus felt about himself and his ministry.

Crucial for my own understanding of what Jesus believed about his ministry is that he saw himself as part of a new world of shared egalitarianism, which was different from the world where worth was determined by status and privilege. In this light, the temptations represent not only the attempt of Satan to get Jesus to misuse his power for selfish, personal gain, they also represent Satan's attempt to pull Jesus away from the shared egalitarian world, back into the current world of inequality and status stratification. Satan's ultimate goal was to get Jesus to abandon the world to come for the present world, but Jesus was smart enough to know what Satan was about.

One way to understand the world in which Jesus lived is to attend to the social dimensions of that world. That world was socially constructed by a people who shared a set of convictions grounded in beliefs, values, meanings, laws, customs, institutions, and rituals.[4] His was the world of first-century Palestinian Judaism, ruled politically by the Roman Empire. It was an agrarian and rural society with several administrative cities.

Borg helps us envisage the social world of Jesus by attending to the dominant assumptions shaping the consciousness of the people of that time.[5] Of great significance is the reconstruction of this world shaped by a shamed-based dynamic. By *shamed-based* I am referring to a class-stratified society oriented toward in-group and out-group value categories. Both Roman society and Judaism had such categories, which Crossan calls a patronal system rooted in honor and shame.

> It was also characterized by an abysmal gulf separating the upper from the lower classes. On one side of that great divide were the Ruler and the Governors, who together made up 1 percent of the population but owned at least half of the land. Also on that same side were three other classes: the Priests, who could own as much as 15 percent of the land; the Retainers, ranging from military generals to expert bureaucrats; and the Merchants, who probably evolved upward from the lower classes but who could end up with considerable wealth and even some political power as well. On the other side were, above all, the Peasants—that vast majority of the population about two-thirds of whose annual crop went to support the upper classes. If they were lucky, they lived at subsistence level, barely able to support family, animals, and social obligations and still have enough for the next year's seed supply.[6]

Artisans formed about 5 percent of the population and were recruited from the dispossessed members of the community. There were even lower classes of people, called the degraded and expendable classes, made up of outcasts such as beggars, outlaws, hustlers, day laborers, and slaves.

In this class-stratified system, a person's worth was value-laden, based on honor and shame. There were those who were considered highly valued, and there were those who were not. Those who were deemed unworthy were the marginalized and disenfranchised. They were the sick, poor, members of the lower classes. To the extent that they internalized their station in life, they saw themselves as worthless and valueless. Those who really mattered were of the upper class, which was only 1 percent of the total population. Those in the lower classes suffered humiliation, and they lacked class status and wealth. There was a value hierarchy. Often the lower classes were economically oppressed and made scapegoats for the upper class's shortcomings.[7] Class evaluations and devaluations determined worth, respectability, and honor. They also determined who was discriminated against and oppressed. In short, ancient society was rooted in economic and social discrimination as well as hierarchical and political differentiation.

THE MIMETIC LESSON

Given this social background, the temptations of Jesus can be viewed as an effort of Satan to pull Jesus back from the new emerging world of economic, social, and political egalitarianism into a socially exclusive, unequal, and discriminatory world. Such an achievement would have derailed Jesus' mission and would have undermined Jesus' confidence in himself. Reversing Jesus' mission would have made Jesus a captive of this world. Such bondage would have destroyed Jesus' personality and sabotaged his mimetic example for all of us. Had Satan succeeded, there would have been no way for us to emulate Jesus' attitude and behavior toward Satan. We would have had to find another way toward liberation from our personal hell.

Evil can be defined as tricking people into exchanging their personal future in the egalitarian, promised reality of God for the shamed-based, stratified world of this present reality. Evil is derailing God's plans for our futures and making us believe that the status quo is all that there is to life. Ted Peters, in his book *Sin: Radical Evil in Soul and Society,* says that one dimension of evil is the effort to steal another's power as a way to survive in this world.[8] Satan hoped to make Jesus change his orientation from the world to come to exclusively this world, as a means of stripping Jesus of his power. This was a subtle but deadly challenge which Jesus met head-on.

Jesus' responses to Satan form the basis for our own response to Satan. "Let this mind be in you, which was also in Christ Jesus." We are called to imitate the mind of Jesus. I call this *minding imitation.* In the first temptation, Satan attempted to get Jesus to make an allegiance to the present world by appealing to his physical needs. Jesus, however, said that life is more than thirst and hunger, and he would not be tricked into believing that he was nothing more than thirst or hunger. Second, Satan attempted to get Jesus to use his gifts toward selfish ends, which is an effort to get Jesus to embrace the nonegalitarian standards of the present world. Jesus refused to do this. Third, and finally, Satan promised Jesus authority over the shame-based culture. Jesus refused to give in to this, and God sent angels to minister to Jesus' needs. He successfully met the challenges. God's salvific intentions for us were left intact.

Taking on the mind of Jesus means that we think of ourselves as more than our physical bodies, that we carefully use our gifts for service purposes, and that we do not accept power and prestige in this shame-based, nonegalitarian society at the cost of the future God has promised us in a radically different world. We live in a nonegalitarian world, but we are not to give our primary allegiance to it. To give our allegiance to this world would not only undermine our future, it would undermine our self-worth and confirm our shame or feeling of being unlovable and uncared for.

The mimetic lesson is that Satan and the forces of this world seek to undo changes for the good. There are forces in the world that attempt to undo liberation, to resist change, and to reverse positive changes. Combating the *forces of reversal* that try to sabotage healing and wholeness is what we learn from Jesus. We learn from Jesus: (1) that our lives are not determined by our past but by the unfolding future of God in the present; (2) that tending to our worldly needs—such as hunger, thirst, and security—alone can derail our efforts toward wholeness; (3) that the seduction of idols such as power, prestige, and status can lead toward the bondage and sabotage of our personalities; and (4) that our true wholeness comes from our relationship with God. Putting our relationship with God first puts everything else in perspective.

RESISTANCE TO CHANGE

There are demonic forces that seek to reverse the changes that lead us to affirm ourselves in a shame-based culture. How these forces manifest themselves is not always external to us. They are not as obvious as Satan coming to us in the same way Satan came to Jesus. Rather, the demons are often internal, and they seek to derail us from inside out, not outside in. Once the shame-based lessons of this world are learned and we internalize our unlovableness, the demonic forces are on automatic pilot. The self-sabotaging dimension that seeks to derail us is called resistance. This is the name that behavioral science gives to such forces. It refers to holding on to the shame-based past and its accompanying aspects because of our anxiety about an unknown future. Because of its predictability, the past is preferred to the future. This section is intended to explore that dynamic world of self-sabotaging resistance as a way to design stories that address the internal world of shame in which we live in today.

Although resistance to change is basic to human nature and is evident throughout human history, our contemporary understanding of resistance is grounded in Freudian psychology. According to Freudian psychology, our primary motivation in life is to resolve the conflict that comes from our effort to satisfy our basic biological needs and the social prohibitions against satisfying those needs. We learn patterns of dealing with this conflict, which become part of our personalities and are classified by diagnostic names. Sometimes these patterns are pathological and nonfunctional and need to be changed. Holding on to these nonfunctional patterns even though they are maladaptive is often preferred. When this holding on comes into play in psychotherapy, resistance is at work. The function of the psychic apparatus of the mind, the ego, is to defend against change or innovation until the person is emotionally ready to make the change. In Freudian oriented psychotherapy, the goal is to work with the person's resistance until the person is emotionally ready for change. If the ego has a premonition that change will be uncomfortable and difficult, it will attempt to sabotage the efforts at change.[9]

The Freudian model of resistance does not help us understand how our relationships with others help to reinforce our reluctance to change. There are, indeed, many social and interpersonal forces helping us resist moving into the future and letting go of certain destructive patterns. One perspective for helping us understand our personal resistance to change is family systems theory. Family systems theory emphasizes that there is constant feedback from the environment to which the individual and family must respond. The family needs to face this feedback with its internal mechanisms operating and incorporate new information in ways that enable each family member to grow and develop. Healthy families function on positive feedback in that they process it in ways that enhance the growth of all of its members. Unhealthy families, however, view feedback negatively and resist taking in new information, particularly if new information challenges existing family patterns. Dysfunctional families conspire with individual family members to resist change and hold on to current patterns of interaction. Not knowing the future, such families prefer the present.

Both Freudian and family systems theory help us to understand the dynamics of resistance and can be drawn on when constructing stories. In addition to these two theories of change is a narrative theory of change. Narrative psychology draws on the insights of both Freudian psychology and family systems, providing a perspective for assisting the writing of stories. Narrative translates resistance into literary plot language and explores how resistance manifests itself through narrative plots.

Plot narratives undergird all of our lives. We all are living out some form of story. These stories have a variety of plots, but these plots seem to be summarized best using Greek and Judeo-Christian categories. These plot categories are comedic, romantic, tragic, ironic, and eschatological.[10] Of significance here are the comedic and tragic plots. One is positive and the other is negative. The comedic plot moves toward a positive end and seems to rule out tragedy. Tragedy moves toward negative ends and does not consider positive possibilities. Romantic plots are unrealistically positive while ironic plots are unrealistically negative. Eschatological plots, however, move toward positive ends, although they move through a series of negative interruptions and setbacks.

From the point of view of resistance, tragedy never envisages a positive end. Rather, resistance is a mode of being that perpetuates a negative story and outcome. In this perspective, resistance assures the negative or tragic outcome.

From the point of view of comedy, resistance is ignored. Setbacks and interruptions in life are evaded and never dealt with creatively. Eschatological plots, which grow out of the Judeo-Christian story, take seriously tragic moments and events and respond to resistance as a real part of life. Unlike comedy, eschatological plots do not ignore resistance. Resistance is something that can be transformed. Unlike tragedy, eschatological plots do not assume that resistance is the last word. Rather, eschatological plots believe that plots thicken or have negative interruptions but also twist or return to their original directional goal.

The kingdom that Jesus inaugurates is eschatological and takes resistance to its manifestation very seriously. Setbacks and thickening of plots are viewed as commonplace, but they are not the final word. Overcoming setbacks and keeping the story of God's kingdom unfolding in its appropriate direction is the hope that undergirds the eschatological vision that Jesus adhered to.

All three of these views of resistance—psychoanalytic or Freudian, family systems theory, and narrative theory—help us understand the dynamics that Jesus faced in the temptations. Strong deterrents to change were part of reality and were powerful. With his life firmly planted in the eschatological, emergent story, Jesus was able to overcome the challenge from Satan and orient his life away from the shame-based, hierarchical and class-stratified society. He kept his vision on the eschatological family that was grounded in an egalitarian ethic.

From Jesus' response to Satan, we decipher how Jesus felt about himself. He saw his very existence as dependent on God and on the coming kingdom. Shame was not possible because his identity was rooted in his relationship to God. He was not dependent on the external shame-based culture that surrounded him. From a biblical point of view, shame is fundamentally giving allegiance to the shame-based ideology that shapes society and internalizing this value system as if it were reality. Whether one is a member of the lower class or the upper class, one's worth is determined by one's orientation. We are presented with at least two possible orientations—God's relationship to us and our relationship to God, on the one hand, and orienting ourselves primarily through cultural expectations, on the other. Orienting ourselves through a relationship to God leads to liberation and to our true identities while orienting ourselves exclusively to societal expectations locks us into a shame and honor ideology that makes our worth dependent on finite values. Jesus was able to defeat and frustrate Satan's efforts because he chose his relationship to God and the coming eschatological and egalitarian community of God. We can emulate Jesus' choice for the future rather than the past or the present. We have the same choices that Jesus had. We can choose the way of an external, shame-based culture, or we can choose a relationship with God and the unfolding egalitarian community of God. Choosing God, we can live in the shame-based culture without becoming part of it. We can participate in the world but be not of the world. In this way we take on the mind of Christ.

RETELLING THE STORY OF THE TEMPTATIONS

I want to retell the story of Jesus' temptations based on the exegetical, pastoral, and theological reflections outlined in the preceding sections. My goal is to communicate to people the mind of Christ with respect to living in a shame-based, status-driven, and hierarchical society. Although our society is different from the patronal system of Jesus' time in that we have a well-developed middle class, we still have a shame-based society in which our value is determined by our class status, position, racial and ethnic identity, and gender. The story of Jesus' temptations helps us visualize how our allegiances help determine how we see our self-worth.

The wilderness is a significant place in the Judeo-Christian tradition. It is a place where natural resources are limited. Water and food are scarce. Shelter from the sun during the day is practically nonexistent, and the nights are cool. Too many days and nights alone in the wilderness would severely strain a normal person's will to survive.

The wilderness is also the place where one cannot ignore confronting one's true self. There are no diversions or distractions there. Moreover, we also confront our true finiteness, or human limitations, and the inadequacy of our own resources. To survive any length of time in the wilderness, we have to discover a higher source of power.

The wilderness is the place where one encounters one's need for God. To negotiate the wilderness, we must be like the children of Israel. We must rely on God's manna for food and God's direction for water. We must follow the cloud by day and the fire by night to keep on course. When we near the end of our time in the wilderness, we must also learn to be a commu-

31

nity in fellowship with God so that the walls of Jericho can come tumbling down.

The wilderness is not only a place where one discovers one's need for God, it is also a setting where we are susceptible to being deceived. All the spiritual forces of the world are at work in the wilderness for either good or ill. The benevolent resources of God are prevalent, but so are the destructive forces of Satan, lying in wait to challenge what God is seeking to do. It is in the wilderness that the spiritual fight between God and Satan rages. Humans are expendable in Satan's mind as Satan seeks to disrupt God's plans. The wilderness is a place of blessing as well as curse.

Satan lies in wait, determining those times and places where we are most vulnerable and susceptible to Satan's influence. Satan feels that we can easily resist satanic powers when we are strong and have natural support systems. Satan is patient and will only make a move when we are weakened and tired.

Jesus was at such a place in his life. He had been fasting and praying for nearly forty days. Satan waited until he knew Jesus had reached the point of physical, emotional, and spiritual exhaustion before intervening. In Satan's mind, Jesus was "ripe for the picking."

Before going into the wilderness, Jesus had received the ultimate affirmation from God. God identified him as a son and declared publicly God's pride in Jesus. God gave him the Spirit as a blessing to do God's work in the world. Satan observed all of this. At this point Satan became even more determined to defeat God's plan for the world. God's affirmation of Jesus only angered Satan.

Satan intervened when he thought Jesus was the most vulnerable. The game plan was to draw Jesus back into the world where Satan's powers dominated. Satan was well aware of the new world that was dawning and that God was in the final stages of establishing God's rule on earth. Satan's strategy was to appeal to Jesus' memory of being part of the physical world and the shame-based culture. Satan hoped that Jesus' memory of his past would overcome his desire to fulfill God's mission. Satan felt that if Jesus made his allegiance to the shame-based world, Jesus would have a shame-based identity that Satan could manipulate.

Satan went to work. The first appeal was to Jesus' hunger and thirst. "Strike the rock," said Satan. "Turn it into bread the way Moses got water from the rock in the wilderness." Jesus replied, "I am aware of your strategy and how you want to derail God's plans for me." "I know," said Jesus, "who I am and whose I am. I know where my resources come from. It is written in Scripture that human beings cannot live on bread alone. I am more than my hunger and my thirst. I will not let you reduce me to my physical nature." Jesus finally said, "I get my nourishment from my relationship to God."

Satan was not yet done, although Satan had lost the first round of the fight. Satan tried another tack and appealed to Jesus' selfish side by telling Jesus, "Look out for number one. Come on back into this world, and benefit from its pleasures. I am sure you remember, Jesus, what this world has to offer you. You have everything; why throw it all away? Come back into this world. Just throw yourself down this mountain. You already know that the angels will keep you safe."

Jesus said, "It is written in Scripture that there is no need to put God to the test. I already know God's care for me. God has already shown me great care and love. There is no way you will get me to exchange what God has in store for me."

Becoming desperate, Satan made one last effort to convince Jesus to return to the old world. Satan showed Jesus all the kingdoms of the world and told Jesus that all the world's power could be his if he would only worship Satan. Satan reminded Jesus that things would be much easier in this world than in the world that was coming. Jesus again drew on Scripture and said, "One should worship only God, and God's future for me is far greater than anything you have to offer me." Then Jesus said, "Satan, be gone; leave my sight." Satan went away. At that moment the angels of God came to minister to Jesus' needs. God came through for Jesus, just as Jesus expected.

RETELLING THE TEMPTATIONS IN CONTEMPORARY LANGUAGE

In preaching I believe that it is not enough to tell biblical stories. It is necessary to tell contemporary stories that help people visualize how the mind of Jesus can work for them. Therefore, it is necessary to delve into our memories of encounters with others to find stories that help us imagine what it means to let the mind that was in Jesus be in us. The following story comes from my own counseling. Of course, the names and facts are altered to protect the confidentiality of my counselee.

Patricia came to pastoral counseling because she was in her seventh week of recovery from alcohol and drug addiction. She was in her early thirties, was married, and the mother of two small children. Her husband came from a family in which the mother was an alcoholic, and he was what some would call an enabler, or a co-dependent, in that he covered up for and cooperated with his mother's addiction. Patricia's addiction completely undermined her belief in her own worth and value, and it contributed to her feelings of unlovability and shame. Her husband also contributed to her shame by reminding her that she was no better than his mother. He had no awareness of his role in his wife's alcoholism.

At the core of Patricia's being was a belief and conviction that she was worthless because she did not have any willpower or control over her addiction. Her shame made her feel completely powerless over her drinking and drug use. Her major fear was that the addiction had a will of its own and would assert itself back into her life at any time. She called it a seed that could germinate at any time—regardless of the right season. For her, anytime could be the right season. Her motivation for coming to counseling, Christian counseling as she called it, was to get spiritual help in facing the demon in her life.

The parabolic goal for Patricia was to take seriously her fear and anxiety about her addiction suddenly overtaking her life again. The second goal was to help Patricia develop a perspective toward her addiction that would help her discover personal and spiritual resources for overcoming her fear. Undergirding her personal belief was the nagging thought that all her work at becoming sober would be for naught.

About six weeks into the counseling process, Patricia had an experience that shocked her terribly. She was driving home after doing some routine errands. She said a very clear voice came to her as she was driving telling her that she should be proud of her accomplishment. She had not taken a drink for about three months, and the voice said she needed to reward herself. The voice said, "You need to celebrate by having a party for yourself. About a mile or two up the road is a package store. Pull in there and have a beer to celebrate your accomplishment."

Patricia said, "I knew immediately that it was Satan. I knew that I was facing my worst fears. What I had dreaded for the last three months suddenly manifested itself. My need for alcohol became severe, and I panicked."

"Something remarkable happened," Patricia said. "I remembered that someone in my Bible study class told me to start quoting scripture when I felt tempted. They said that Jesus quoted scripture when he faced the devil. So I began to quote the Lord's Prayer. After quoting it, I felt somewhat better, but the Satan was still there. It was as if he were right there in the car with me, sitting right by my side, trying to get a hold of the steering wheel. I still felt helpless and vulnerable. Then I quoted the Twenty-third Psalm. When I got to the words 'I will fear no evil: for thou art with me,' I felt Satan's presence leave me. I felt relieved, and the crisis was over. I know my testing is not over, but I am glad to know that I have an ally in God when Satan gets to me that way again."

CONCLUDING REMARKS

The story told above actually took place in a pastoral counseling session. Patricia brought a fear into counseling at the beginning that she was weak and could not resist the urge to have a drink. She believed she would regress once challenged. However, she discovered spiritual resources on which she could draw in a time of danger.

People bring certain beliefs about themselves to worship and to counseling. Often the beliefs die very slowly. The story of Jesus resisting temptation and Patricia overcoming temptation are both stories that can be told when trying to address people's shame. Shame undermines self-confidence, and shame holds on in our lives tenaciously. Like a satanic force it tries to prevent us from moving constructively within our lives and seeks to draw us back into the shame-based world. Telling these two stories in the context of preaching or in pastoral counseling has the goal of deconstructing negative convictions about ourselves.

On one occasion I built a sermon around Luke 4:16-30, in which Jesus was rejected by his own community. I entitled the sermon "Overcoming Rejection." The emphasis was that it was a shame-based community that did not believe anything positive could come out of its midst and that therefore rejected Jesus because of its own peasant nature. The rejection of Jesus by his own could have undermined Jesus' self-confidence. I tried to look at what Jesus did and felt about himself in order to find out what helped him deal with rejection. I told the story of the temptations, highlighting Jesus' use of Scripture and his relationship with God. I concluded the sermon with the story of Patricia, emphasizing the importance of emulating Jesus' methods of overcoming shame in the midst of temptation. The goal of using both biblical and contemporary stories is to help people in the congregation to visualize how it is possible to develop the mind that was in Jesus.

The story of Jesus' temptations and Patricia's temptation can be used as parabolic stories to challenge negative self-beliefs. They can help us deal with our reluctance and resistance to change based on our fear of change and our lack of self-confidence.

CHAPTER TWO

CAN ANYTHING GOOD
COME FROM THIS SIDE
OF THE TRACKS?

When a particular group is devalued in a culture, it is hard to imagine that anything positive or extraordinary could come from that group. In fact, disbelief and ridicule seem to come from those within the group as well as from those without. Those who live within the stigmatized group internalize the negative images of the group, and those who are outside the group reenforce the negative images through their attitudes and position. Most devastating are the ways people in devalued groups internalize negative values and form their group identity. Such internalizations become the basis of personal and group identities and follow individuals and groups throughout their lives. The question is, How do people in devalued groups in shame-based cultures overcome the negative stereotypes that are foisted on them and that they internalize? The answer to this question will be sought in this chapter by attending to Jesus' own self-understanding and the way he and his family overcame the shame surrounding his life. Mimetic implications for how we can overcome our own shame will also be explored.

> Is not this the carpenter, the son of Mary, the brother of James, and Joses, and of Juda, and Simon? and are not his sisters here with us? And they were offended at him. (Mark 6:3; cf. Matt. 13:55 and Luke 4:22)

This verse in Mark forms the basis of the tradition of Jesus' rejection by his own community. The significance of this passage is that it represents the resistance to Jesus from his own community based on the community's internalized shame grounded in their social status. Crossan's book comments on the social status of Jesus' community:

> Ramsay MacMullen has noted that one's social pedigree would easily be known in the Greco-Roman world and that a description such as "carpenter" indicated lower-class status. At the back of his book he gives a "Lexicon of Snobbery" filled with terms used by literate and therefore upper-class Greco-Roman authors to indicate their prejudice against illiterate and therefore lower-class individuals. Among those terms is *tekton*, or "carpenter," the same term used for Jesus in Mark 6:3 and for Joseph in Matthew 13:55.... In general, the great divide in the Greco-Roman world was between those who had to work with their hands and those who did not.[1]

Jesus belonged to the lower class, and confronted with what his community heard about his achievements, people in Nazareth had difficulty accepting his reputation. They found it hard to believe that a person of Jesus' low status could achieve notoriety, which was traditionally reserved for those with wealth, status, and position. The naysayers were people from Jesus' own class, and this raises a profound concern for how shame becomes internalized by the group that is stigmatized. If Jesus' own group is so stigmatized, how did he himself escape such internalizations of shame? What made him different?

From the standpoint of the cultural background of Jesus, he was a woodworker, a member of a peasant society.[2] Agrarian peasants were at the lower end of the economic ladder and produced goods and services for the city or state, as well as for themselves. In this community Jesus is a woodworker. Meier comments on Jesus' occupation.

> Jesus would have made various pieces of furniture, such as beds, tables, stools, and lampstands (2 Kgs 4:10), as well as boxes, cabinets, and chests for storage. Justin Martyr claims that Jesus also made "plows and yokes." While this is probably an inference by Justin rather than a relic of oral tradition, it does tell us what work a person from Palestine—which Justin was—would attribute to a *tekton*.[3]

Jesus was poor and had to work for a living. He had no claim to status and position. Thus, it was extremely difficult for those in Jesus' community, rich or poor, to fathom Jesus' reputation. "Surely," they said, "this can't be. Is not this the carpenter and a son of a carpenter? Don't we know this family? A person of such origin surely cannot have risen to such a place of honor."

It is very clear that people of the lower class knew their position and status in society. This appears to have been detrimental to their self-esteem or feelings of self-worth. Relying on status or position for self-estimation and self-worth could lead people in Jesus' day to have very low self-regard, yet it appears that Jesus completely escaped such feelings. He seemed to have transcended the conventional standards of his day that might have led him to crippling self-deprecation. The question is, How did Jesus escape the detrimental aspects of self-hatred that seem to characterize those of the community in which he was born and reared?

It is important to explore just how people in Jesus' home community could have developed this negative attitude and why it did not affect Jesus. It is important to use our contemporary understanding of the internalization of shame in order to decipher how low status and position turn into shame.[4]

THE INTERNALIZATION OF SHAME

Jesus' response to rejection in the passages noted indicates clearly that there is no clinical or psychological evidence for believing that Jesus suffered from a shame-based personality. A shame-based personality internalizes the negative images of one's group identity, such images undermining one's basic sense of well-being. It is possible to argue that Jesus had consistently been exposed to shame and humiliating situations throughout his adult ministry, but it seems that he never suffered from internalization of shame.

From the perspective of depth psychology, shame in a shame-based adult personality has early antecedents in childhood. Gershen Kaufman argues that scenes of shame early in a child's life have the potential of shaping how that person experiences shame in adulthood. Memories of our basic interpersonal needs being frustrated and the failure of meeting these needs lead to feelings of being humiliated, unloved, and shamed.[5] A certain meaning is attributed to such shame-filled memories, and it later shapes any subsequent experience of shame. All succeeding experiences of shame are seen from the point of view of the memory of the original shaming event. Kaufman says that powerful experiences of humiliation in a child's early life are accompanied by strong, negative interpretations of oneself and a negative narrative or script for behavior based on the negative interpretations of self. Such powerful scenes are activated in subsequent experiences of shame, as the person relives the original shaming event. The original scenes of humiliation that shape subsequent experiences of shame Kaufman calls *governing scenes*.

In his earthly ministry Jesus consistently faced rejection, ridicule, and hostility in his interpersonal and group encounters. His responses to these humiliating events were usually without what is called *delusions of self-reference*—meaning he never took them personally. This was ultimately expressed in his memorable words from the cross, "Father, forgive them; for they know not what they do" (Luke 23:34). Had Jesus suffered from a shame-based personality, he would not have been able to transcend the humiliation he suffered or be concerned about others. He would have been wrapped up in himself.

Jesus' transcending responses to humiliation and rejection throughout his life tell us that there was no governing scene of shame in his life. This means that there were dynamics at work early in his life that caused him to reinterpret scenes of humiliation in growth facilitating ways. From the point of view of interpersonal relationships, this means that the parental rearing practices surrounding Jesus' upbringing were extremely effective and that Jesus himself had some internal spiritual dimension that aided him as he confronted humiliation. Our concern is to explore some historical reconstructions about Jesus' early life in order to discern just why Jesus handled humiliating experiences the way he did. Discerning the reasons for his responses to shame-filled experiences may give us a clue of how we too can take on the mind of Jesus.

CHARACTERISTICS OF JESUS

Jesus had the uncanny ability for realistic appraisal of himself and others. One of the dimensions of a shame-based personality is the inability to separate one's own view of reality from the views of others. The person seems to be engulfed within the attitudes and expectations of others. Jesus seems to have been free from absorption in the expectations of others and able to separate his own view of things from those of others. This ability is known as *self-differentiation,* and it requires the person to develop a sense of self apart from others. Self-differentiation also demands a fair amount of self-esteem and awareness of one's own inner motivation and aspirations.

In the context of his home community, self-differentiation meant that he did not need to make excuses for their rejection. He did not need to take it personally. Rather, he could accept it for what it was without having to deceive himself. Their approval of him was important, but on the inside he had what it took to live, despite the rejection. Having their approval was not essential to the survival of his personality or his ministry. Their respect or honor for him was not mandatory for his self-esteem.

The rejection did have some influence on him, however. He was not able to do very much ministry among his own people. They were not open to opportunities for their own growth and development, and Jesus saw no need to force what he had to offer on them. He left them free to respond in whatever way they saw fit. This respect for others, which let them make their own decisions about what they wanted in life, was a central dimension of Jesus' ministry and represents the height of self-differentiation and maturity.

THE SOURCES OF JESUS' SELF-DIFFERENTIATION

The factors that led to Jesus' realistic appraisal of himself had spiritual and parental sources. The spiritual sources involved self-understanding of his relationship to God, and the parental sources related to the child-rearing practices that assisted in the development of his self-differentiation.

Jesus' self-referral as a rejected prophet is significant for understanding his spiritually. In Mark 6:4 Jesus compares himself to a prophet, and in Luke 4:18-24 Jesus identifies himself as part of the prophetic tradition by identifying himself with the words of Isaiah.[6] Jesus brought to his adult ministry a profound sense of vocation and ministry. Such a significant awareness was basic to his ability to respond to rejection without self-deprecation. The sense of mission and purpose in life is a central distinguishing factor in moving forward in life despite rejection. Having a sense of calling pulled Jesus away from and set him apart from his family, his peers, and his community. It is from God, who called him, that he ultimately received his ability to transcend rejection.

Perhaps the offense that Jesus' kin felt was related to his sense of mission and purpose in life. Their offense could have been a defense against their own shame or their own inability to affirm a sense of calling. Resenting others who have embraced their own calling is often a sign of one's refusal to accept one's own calling. To accept a call may mean losing the support of one's community. Some even give up the call in order not to be alienated from the community.

This insight comes from further application of self-differentiation theory. Self-distinguishing in dysfunctional families often is accompanied by rejection.[7] Dysfunctional families are generally families who find it hard to allow family members to develop their own uniqueness and differentness; in contrast, functional families facilitate such self-differentiation. Those who insist on being themselves and developing their own unique identities are often viewed as outsiders and are seen as betrayers in dysfunctional families. Jesus was a member of a dysfunctional community that had difficulty with his ability to self-differentiate. They forced him from his home and community. Luke 4:29-30 says they sought to do him bodily harm by throwing him out of town.

Refusal to accept one's call for fear of rejection produces shame. It is the humiliation associated with not fulfilling one's internal image of God. Conversely, accepting one's call is a basic source of real self-esteem, which becomes part of the ability to overcome rejection. Jesus survived rejection because he had developed the capacity for self-differentiation. His self-differentiation was rooted in his call.

A second factor in handling rejection has to do with the way

Jesus was raised. He was raised in a family that from the very conception of Jesus learned to handle shame graciously. Jesus learned from his parents that there is no shame in carrying out the purposes of God. From the point of view of Jesus' community, his mother, Mary, was pregnant out of wedlock. This was a shameful development that had the potential of being ridiculed by the community. However, Jesus' parents saw God at work in the whole birth process, and the birth narrative became a main source for Jesus' self-understanding and ministry.

Our understanding of birth narratives comes from modern psychology. In her book *The Birth of the Living God,* Anna-Maria Rizzuto talks about the significance of birth stories, which are also important in understanding how Jesus overcame rejection.[8]

A brief review of Rizzuto's theory of birth story may be helpful. For our purposes I will take her conclusions out of her psychoanalytic, or Freudian, cast and put them into a narrative psychological framework. In such a framework, wish-fulfillment is no longer envisaged as the motivation for the creation of birth stories, as when parents' fantasies about having children shape reality. Rather, the emphasis in narrative psychology is on a family bringing meaning to an event that, in turn, links the child to a significant historical reality that forms the basis of the child's later self-understanding.

Rizzuto points out that a child is born into a world that is already shaped with ideas and expectations. There are certain expectations that parents have of their children, and some of these expectations include God representations or God images, which later inform the lives of their children. She attributes the origin of these God images to the mind and imagination of the parents. In these attributions the child is often envisaged as a gift from God, a punishment imposed, or a tribulation sent by God to test the parent. These ideas are transmitted to the child in Rizzuto's mind by storytelling, which subtly conveys what kind of intervention by God brought the child into existence. Such ideas become the birth mythology that later develops into the child's own image of God and informs his or her belief in self and self-worth or value.[9]

Drawing on the significance of Rizzuto's birth mythology, it is important to examine the stories Jesus was told about his own birth. Although there is no evidence that Jesus was told any of the birth stories that now appear in the synoptic Gospels, it may be possible to reconstruct from Jesus' adult life the birth stories he was told. Here a modification of the criterion of rejection and execution is used to do the reconstruction. This criterion does not decide which of Jesus' experiences are historical, but it does point to the fact of Jesus' rejection and humiliation throughout his ministry and tries to explain how he was able to handle them.[10] One way to explain his ability to handle rejection and humiliation is to point to the parental training that he might have received. Birth stories are concrete ways that parents give their children a sense of meaning and purpose in life.

We do have the actual birth stories recorded in Matthew and Luke. Whether Jesus' parents and community actually used these stories is not known, for we have virtually no material about Jesus' childhood. It is plausible to conclude that Jesus was told some kind of stories about his conception and birth, unless the circumstances of his birth were a secret and a source of shame. I contend that the historical Jesus would have been adversely influenced had his birth stories been hidden from him. He would not have had the ability to transcend humiliation had his birth stories been a source of shame. Contemporary family systems theory tells us of the negative impact that family secrets have on personality development.[11]

Moving away from wish-fulfillment theory, we observe that Mary is pictured in Matthew and Luke as the historical fulfillment of the expectations of an entire faith community (Matt. 1:18-25; Luke 2:1-20). It is not unusual for parents to have expectations for their children even before they are born, according to Rizzuto. That Matthew and Luke and perhaps Jesus' parents might have expressed such expectations from the perspective of the history of faith is not unusual either. This was an ancient, as well as a contemporary, practice. My own research on the birth myths of pastors indicates that many of them were born with religious expectations of some form or another, which shaped their responses to life.[12]

Matthew talks about the shame attached to Jesus' conception. Joseph, being a just man who was unwilling to put Mary to shame, had resolved to divorce her quietly. Matthew says an angel appeared to Joseph in a dream and told him that she had conceived by the Holy Spirit and he should call the child Jesus, for he would save the world from its sins (Matt. 1:19-21). This was viewed as the fulfillment of an ancient prophecy. In Luke, the angel appeared to Mary and told her she had been favored by God and that she would conceive and bear a son who should be called Jesus (Luke 1:26-35). These two Gospels have elaborate birth stories that are not wish-fulfillment, as Rizzuto has defined wish fulfillment. Rather, they represent religious expectations for the coming of a messiah, a messiah who had been promised in the Hebrew Scripture and who the New Testament writers felt was fulfilled in Jesus.

From the point of view of the Jesus of history debate, the facts of the conception of Jesus are not as important as the actual birth story and the impact that it may have had on Jesus himself. We agree with Rizzuto that birth stories have a profound impact on the child who is told the birth story. It shapes the reality of the child and the child's view of God and the world. Thus, if Jesus was told of his conception and the expectations regarding it, which is completely plausible given the world in which Jesus was reared, his self-understanding could have been shaped very early.

Whether or not one subscribes to the Virgin Birth, there had to be an account of Jesus' conception out of wedlock. The way Matthew and Luke accounted for the premarital conception would surely have countered any shame that Mary, Joseph, or Jesus might have had. Thus, from a purely historical perspective, had Mary and Joseph told Jesus about their theological views of his conception, he would have internalized a sense of being special and significant.

Because we have contemporary accounts of birth stories or stories about people's conception, their time in the womb, their birth, and the shaping power of their childhood, we can speculate that Jesus was greatly influenced by the stories he was told about his birth. Knowing what we know about Jesus' adult ministry and life, we can conclude that he must have been shaped in a positive way by the stories his parents told him of his conception and birth. Taking his nature as fully human, we need to understand how his identity and mission were formed and shaped by his parents and his community.

The stories that I will retell about Jesus emphasize the point that birth stories told by his parents helped him see the circumstances of his birth in a shameless way. The mimetic implication for us is that we too can help parents shape the world of their own children by placing the birth of their children in God's unfolding story of salvation.

RETELLING
BIRTH STORIES IN PREACHING
AND COUNSELING

Early Lessons in Overcoming Shame

In this storytelling section I will draw on the actual historical material of Jesus' life as it has been recorded in the Gospels. I will, however, make Jesus' mother, Mary or Miriam, the primary narrator in order to introduce the historical material in an imaginative storytelling way. The point of the story is to introduce to parents the role of child-rearing practices that will enable children to reframe potentially humiliating events that might happen to them. The stories can also be used to help adults who lived difficult childhoods to discern how God may be at work in them healing them.

While we know very little about the actual parenting skills of Jesus' parents, there is enough evidence from the child-rearing practices of the community in which Jesus grew up to make the story related below plausible. It is obvious that two of the Gospel writers reported Jesus' conception and birth in a way that took away the humiliation of being conceived without benefit of marriage. The following story assumes that Mary had the reframing talent to help her son come to grips with the circumstances of his conception and birth.

Jesus returned home one afternoon from instruction in the synagogue with a hurt and despondent look on his face. Mary asked him, "What on earth is the matter with you. You look so down. Please tell me what has happened." "Well, Mother," said Jesus, "it kind of hurts for me to talk to you about it. It is very embarrassing, and I should keep it to myself. It really is not something that is good to talk about at all." "Please," said Mary, "it is too heavy a burden to keep something that important to you pent up inside. You need to share it. This is the best thing." "All right Mother, I will share it with you although I still think it is not a good idea."

Jesus went on to tell his mother how he had been teased in school about the circumstances of his birth. He said "The kids at school began to tease me, saying that Joseph is not my father. I didn't let them know that I was hurt hearing this, since I knew they were trying to upset me. I knew that eventually I would find out the truth so I said nothing to them."

"I see," said Mary with a voice of empathic concern. "This is indeed a difficult thing for your ears to hear. Let me set the record straight so that you will know the truth and never have to wonder again about such matters."

Mary began to tell Jesus his birth story. "Jesus your conception was not ordinary, but it was by no means anything sinful, as your so-called friends tried to imply. True enough, I was not married to your father, nor had I had sexual relationships with any other man. Children normally come from the union between a husband and a wife. An angel appeared to me and told me the things that were about to happen to me. The angel told me that I would conceive you by the power of the Holy Spirit and that I should call your name Jesus. As you can believe, I had all kinds of reservations about this, knowing that people in the community would have a great deal of difficulty believing me. The angel assured me that everything would be all right and this was all God's intended plan. Through you, Jesus, the angel said that God would redeem the world."

Jesus responded to his mother, "You are saying, Mother, that my conception was by the hand of God." Mary responded, "Not only this, but I was told to name you Jesus by the angel. I realized sometime later that the name Jesus is a very important name in our Hebrew faith."[13] Mary continued, "I am telling you this because I know you are of the age to understand these things. Your synagogue friends don't really understand, and they see your conception as something shameful and humiliating. Yes, even your father Joseph himself wondered at first about it, but the angel spoke to him as well. He too got excited about what you would mean to us and to God's future."

Mary went on to tell Jesus that not only was his conception extraordinary, his birth was as well. She told him about not having enough room in the inn and how he was born in a stable. She told him how men from foreign lands heard about the birth of a new king and saw a star in the east signaling that a new age had been born. She told him that although they were not from the same religious tradition, they knew this was an important sign of the time.

Mary then went on to tell about his dedication at the temple and how the old priest looked at Jesus and claimed to be ready to die because his eyes had seen the salvation of the world. Mary concluded her talk with Jesus with the following response. "You see Jesus, there is nothing to be ashamed of because God was involved in your conception and your birth from the very beginning."

As you can see from this story re-creation, Jesus could have been taught by his family how to deal with potentially shameful situations. This was done primarily by reframing the events in light of God's story of salvation.

This story can be told in preaching and pastoral counseling with people who bring shamed-based memories of their conceptions and birth. It could also be helpful for parents who have conceived children out of wedlock or in oppressive situations and who wonder about how it may affect their children. There is a strong theological tradition that believes that conceptions are no accident and that God has a purpose for each person who has been conceived.

A Contemporary Birth Story

We only know our birth myths or stories because we are told of them by others. They are about our conception, time in the womb, and the first year following our birth. They are important because they tell us about whether we are welcome or unwelcome in this world.[14] Therefore, it is important to help people who have negative or unwelcoming birth myths deal with issues of shame and humiliation that might have accompanied their birth and the possible way this might have undermined their self-esteem. This can be done by helping such people reframe their birth stories in light of God's overall purposes. Rebecca's story is a case in point.

Rebecca felt that she was unwanted and unloved. She never quite felt she really was wanted by her mother. Because of this, she did everything she could to make herself acceptable to her mother. She never gave her mother any trouble. She became a model human being. Yet, she had one big flaw as an adult. She found that her need to please was carried over into her relationships with men. She found she could not say no to their sexual advances. As a result she felt she lacked a good sense of who she was.

When Rebecca was at one of her lowest points, she mustered enough courage to ask her mother about her conception and her birth. Her mother responded openly about them. Her feeling unwanted was well founded, her mother told her. Rebecca's mother had had a very shaky relationship with Rebecca's father and did not want to be pregnant at all. She told her how depressed she had been because she had become pregnant by a man she did not love. They married when she found out she was pregnant, and the pregnancy brought nothing but difficulty to them.

Rebecca continued her story and said that her mother told her something that made all the difference in the world. Rebecca's mother told her that the first time she laid eyes on her she felt blessed by God and that she loved her the instant she saw her. Rebecca knew then that she was wanted despite the circumstances of her conception and birth.

Rebecca wished she had had the courage to ask her mother about the story earlier. She felt she had gone through a lot of agony and pain unnecessarily. Her mother's revelation set the stage for her to see herself and her life as a gift from God. It enabled her to be more accepting of herself and to set some personal boundaries.

CONCLUDING REMARKS

Jesus learned how to deal with shame because of his parents' initiative in helping him know his birth story. Although this is speculation, there is evidence that Jesus' name meant something important. Also, the Gospel writers did some reframing of their own. Helping people see their conception and birth as part of God's salvation plan makes a great deal of difference in how they handle shame.

CHAPTER THREE

PARENTAL REJECTION

"My God, my God, why hast thou forsaken me?"
(MATTHEW 27:46 and MARK 15:34)

"Father, forgive them; for they know not what they do."
(LUKE 23:34)

In her controversial book *Sisters in the Wilderness,* Delores Williams severely challenges the atonement formulation that focuses on God's sacrifice of God's son, Jesus.[1] She calls this God's child abuse. She says that such an inhumane formulation is detestable and needs to be rethought and couched in a less harmful doctrine.

It would be the ultimate tragedy if, indeed, God were a child abuser. Such a possibility rails against everything I know and have experienced God to be. Yet, I know that there are those who believe God to be an abusive and punitive parent. In Greek mythology the tragic heroine or hero is one who places confidence in a god only to come to realize that this confidence is misplaced. In Greek mythology the gods are only concerned about their agenda, not the personal welfare of humans.

The ultimate shame, and one from which it is almost impossible to recover, is the feeling that one is unloved by God. The root of shame, according to Leon Wurmser, is believing that one is unlovable and will never be loved.[2] If such a humiliating conclusion is true from God's perspective, then there is no ground for hope at all.

Cultural despisers of religion rejoice in the possible conclusion that the current abuse of children might have its roots in God's sacrifice of God's son. Even the words of Jesus on the cross, "My God, my God, why hast thou forsaken me?" sound as if Jesus confirms this conclusion himself. It seems that Matthew and Mark also confirm the notion of an abusive parent.

The question might be asked, Is not this a double humiliation for Jesus? Is not his mocking while on the cross and his rejection by his own Father a double dose of unbearable rejection? Certainly Jesus' ability to handle rejection in his early life and in his ministry were grounded largely in his fundamental belief that there was nothing that could separate him from God's love.

The question that gives shape to this chapter centers on whether Jesus actually believed he was abandoned by God while he was on the cross. The question is, Was what Jesus said on the cross an expression of his feeling of abandonment, or was it a complaint or lamentation addressed to God that led to faith in God?

Many people bring to church and to pastoral counseling a belief that God has abandoned and forsaken them. They are convinced that there is no possible way that God could actually love or care for them. Deep down inside they harbor a thief who is robbing them of their self-esteem and a hopeful outlook on life. A thief who sabotages self-esteem and robs people of hope is not easily removed from the center of one's life. The removal of the thief requires the divine help of God as well as the committed cooperation of those who believe that God has abandoned them.

There are those who have actually been abandoned, neglected, or ignored by their parents. Some of these blame God for this lack of parental caring. Many are convinced that God could not care less about what happens to them. They interpret Jesus' words of being forsaken on the cross as the act that finally confirmed God's true, noncaring nature. They see themselves suffering the ultimate shame of being unlovable, and it is all God's doing, in their minds. Any God who would abandon God's own child would have no qualms about abandoning others.

The real historical and human Jesus is portrayed in this chapter raising a question that all of us at some time have raised or will raise if we live long enough. What Jesus actually believed about God is very important. The point that will be presented is that the real Jesus was not expressing a belief but was actually expressing a complaint that all humans express to God. Such a complaint or lament is a first step toward faith and confessing the goodness of God. It is in the expression of our complaint that God responds to us to show us how God really cares. God shows this care through an actual divine presence to the one feeling abandoned, and the abandonment disappears. God is at God's best when we are able to let God know our feelings, just as Jesus was able to do.

JESUS' HUMANNESS ON THE CROSS

The words that Jesus spoke on the cross reveal his complete humanness to the point of complaining about God's lack of presence in his life. Exactly what Jesus meant by his final words of complaint against God will be our goal.

Mark and Matthew have a similar account of Jesus' complaint against God (Mark 15:34 and Matt. 27:46). Luke 23:46 has Jesus expressing trust in God rather than a complaint. The critical question is, How is it possible to account for Matthew and Mark's account of Jesus' complaint about God? Is Jesus' complaint an expression of Jesus' desperation, revealing Jesus' belief that God had completely abandoned him? Are those who believe that God abused Jesus by sacrificing him correct? Or, is the complaint against God the first stage in a process of reaffirmation of faith in God as a good and loving Father?

The answers to these varied but related questions can be found by identifying the origins of the words that Jesus spoke on the cross near the end of his life. These words, expressed in Mark and Matthew, are commonly believed to be from the first verse of Psalm 22. The words Jesus expressed in Luke come from Psalm 31:5.

The structure of these two different psalms is very important in answering the questions that have been raised. Psalm 31 is made up of several independent psalms.[3] Verses 1-6 are a psalm of trust, including the words in verse 5, "Into thy hand I commit my spirit" (RSV). Verse 9 starts the individual lament or complaint against God, and verses 19-24 make up a complete individual psalm of praise. Even though Psalm 31 is the combination of several different types of psalms, they have come to us as a unit, expressing both praise of God and lament or complaint against God.

Psalm 22 in its entirety is a psalm of lament with a reversal built into its structure. In this psalm, praise follows lament.[4] The complaint is that God is distant. It is an abandonment complaint against God. In verses 1-2 the suppliant's complaint goes un-heeded by God, but the relationship between God and the sup-pliant is evident.[5] In verse 3 God remains silent, but the paradox is that God is present all the time. In verses 4-5 the complaint shifts to a memory of God's helping God's people; in verse 6-8 the suffering has not yet been relieved; in verses 9-11 the suppli-ant reviews a personal relationship with God, revealing God com-ing closer and closer to the suppliant; and finally, there is a movement from lament to petition. In verses 22-31 the reversal is complete as the suppliant praises God.[6]

The point of this is to highlight that neither Psalm 31 nor Psalm 22 is a personal expression of distrust in God. These psalms are not final testaments to an abusive God. They are, rather, profound testimonies of trust in God at the ultimate extreme of life. They are human expressions of the soul's move-ment from complaint to confession of faith. They represent a movement similar to what behavioral sciences say we go through during the death, dying, and bereavement processes. Donald Capps in his book *Biblical Approaches to Pastoral Care* points out that the psalms of lament have structures and patterns similar to the grief patterns that people go through.[7] Thus, to interpret Jesus' words, "My God, my God, why hast thou forsaken me?" as an expression of distrust in an abusive God is absurd.

SHAME AND THE PSALMS

There are fifty psalms of lament within the one hundred fifty psalms. They enable us to confront our shame, vulnerability, and humiliation and express our feelings about them. The psalms of lament take seriously our hurt and anger over our ridicule and abuse at the hands of others. They realize that God is the appro-priate One to whom to express our consternation about the real-ity of suffering in life. They help us give expression to our feelings about our unlovability and our not receiving care. The wisdom of the psalms of lament is that deep feelings of frustration and agony cannot remain unexpressed without doing serious damage to the one who has them. Pastoral theologians—such as John Patton, in his book *Is Human Forgiveness Possible?*—have talked about the dev-astating effects of shame denied by individuals.

Obviously the historical Jesus knew the Psalms and used them in moments of complete vulnerability. Whether Jesus quoted the whole psalm aloud within the hearing of those witnessing the crucifixion is not stated. It is obvious from the words that he used from Psalms 22 and 31 that he had them in mind and was perhaps reciting them quietly to himself before he came to what he had to say out loud. What can be said is that he moved from lament or complaint to confession of trust in God. He felt the reversal of mood. Commenting on the role of God in the Psalms, Westermann says:

> The center of all the Old Testament's theological discourse is found in a verbal clause: God has acted. That can only be said by one who has actually experienced what God has done, in this case the speaker in Psalm 22. His experience has been shaped by the contrast which determines the progression of the Psalm from its first to last verse. Only because he had experienced God's remoteness and God's silence could he experience their reversal; and because he had experienced this reversal, he had to recount it.[8]

Psalms of lament enable us to confront our vulnerability, shame, and humiliation and to express them. Psalms of lament take seriously our hurt and anger over being ridiculed and mocked. We can neither run away nor ignore our deepest feelings of being uncared for and unloved. The wisdom of the psalms of lament is that deep feelings of agony over the presence of suffering in life can be confronted and expressed without negative sanctions.

Pastoral theologians and pastoral psychologists tell us how devastating it can be to deny and keep from our awareness our feelings of shame and humiliation. John Patton goes through a series of negative results that the denial of shame can have on the development of personality.[9] He draws on psychoanalytic, object relations, and self psychology traditions to show that denied shame takes the center stage and cripples personality growth. The wisdom of these psychological traditions is their emphasis on the unconscious hypothesis. From the perspective of these three traditions, much of human awareness runs at the deepest levels of the human mind, shaping and determining behavior. The way the ego functions to prevent us from being overwhelmed by shame requires elaborate defenses. Recent shame psychology, which is an outgrowth of these psychoanalytic traditions, shows that we take into ourselves the original shame event and shame scenes as a means of defending ourselves against them. What is taken in is remembered and becomes the organizing and governing memory for future encounters with shameful events and people.[10] The problem with internalizing shame to control shame is that it makes the shameful event and its remembrance a permanent part of the self. It then becomes an internal saboteur of personal worth and self-esteem.

Psalms of lament attempt to undermine the internalization of shame. They help us become aware of the shame we feel and give expression to it. Putting into words our shame prevents us from having to hold on to these feelings. It is only when feelings are *not* expressed that we swallow shame. Swallowing shame is what creates the internal problem in the first place.

On the cross Jesus did not swallow his shame. He expressed his shame through the recitation of Psalms 22 and 31. These psalms helped prevent him from internalizing his shame. He had a safety valve, which enabled him to process the shame he underwent through the use of lament and complaint.

MIMETIC IMPLICATIONS

The mimetic implication of mimicking Jesus is obvious. We too must not swallow our shame, but we must express it. I belong to a devalued ethnic group. Shame is triggered any time I or any member of my ethnic and racial group is devalued. Some people say that perhaps we are too sensitive and should not be so quick to name something as racism or prejudice. Moreover, in days not too far gone, we would use the mechanism of testimonies within the African American church tradition to talk openly about the shame we encountered as a way to keep from swallowing the shame. Frankly confronting the shame and not swallowing it enabled Jesus to carry our shame. We can truly say with the Negro spiritual, "Nobody knows the trouble I see, nobody knows but Jesus." The words could be easily changed to "Nobody knows the shame I feel, nobody but Jesus." Complaints about racism and testimonies of the shame we encounter are safety valves against swallowing shame. They are very similar to the psalms of lament in that they express our feelings of shame and humiliation, which become opportunities for God's healing.

A CONTEMPORARY STORY OF EXPRESSING SHAME

After I had preached about shame, a woman who had been sexually molested by her father came to me crying with joy. She said that for many years she had hidden from herself and everyone else the fact that she had been sexually molested. She said that she denied the experiences ever happened. She kept it a secret for nearly forty years and never allowed herself to face the truth about her father's exploitation of her.

For a long time, she continued saying, the hidden secret determined her life. It prevented her from having the kind of closeness she wished she could have with others. She grew distant from her mother and siblings. She entered into a series of abusive relationships. She had a failed marriage, and she was not as effective a parent as she knew she could have been. She said she often wondered when things went wrong in her life.

She said that as she listened to the sermon, it became very clear what she had been doing. She did not feel she could ever face head-on the shameful event that happened to her. She blamed herself and felt really guilty for what had happened. But, something about the Gospel framing the issue of shame enabled her to confront her secret. She was able to recall the governing shame-scene, and this finally brought healing in her life. She was crying because the scales had fallen suddenly from her eyes, the way they fell from Paul's eyes when Ananias touched them on the street called Straight.

Throughout my ministry I have encountered people who have had criminally shameful acts happen to them. They have kept these events secretly inside, swallowing them. The event itself was devastating, but it also left negative boot prints and open, festering wounds on the person's life. Only when they allowed others to know what had happened and made the shame external to

MOVING FROM SHAME TO SELF-WORTH

themselves did the wounds begin to heal and a scab begin to form over the open wound.

RETELLING THE STORY OF THE CRUCIFIXION

Some people's shame is so deep that it is not possible for them to envision themselves as part of God's plan. They see no way out of their predicament. Sometimes I find myself telling Bible stories that I feel make sense in their situation. One story is as follows.

There was one witness to the crucifixion that you don't hear much about. We don't have much information about him at all. All we know is that he was an official guard placed there to watch the crowd during the crucifixion of Jesus. Have you ever wondered what he might have seen and what he might have reported to contemporary reporters?

There is a song that asks, "Were you there when they crucified my Lord?" Well, the centurion can say, "Yes." If he were to tell his story, he probably would recount the story in the following way.

Yes, I was there all the time. I witnessed the entire sad event. Initially, it was a very disturbing event. I observed the governor's feast where it was customary to release a criminal. The crowd was gathered, and they seemed unusually excited. I had witnessed this kind of behavior once before. It was at a time when there was going to be a government execution. They must have known that there might be a possible execution; they were anticipating the excitement of seeing blood, particularly innocent blood, spilt.

Pilot asked the crowd what he should do with Barabbas? They shouted, "Release him!" Pilot then asked what he should do with Jesus? They said, "Crucify him!" During all this time, Jesus never said a mumbling word, not a word. He did not even defend himself.

I saw the whole battalion of soldiers strip him naked, place a crown of thorns on his head, and put a reed in his right hand. It did not happen to me, but I felt the humiliation that Jesus must have felt. I said to myself, "No man should ever have to go through this." They were saying things like, "Go ahead and

58

save yourself. You say you are the new messiah; well if you are, save yourself." Their laughter was deafening.

I was also there when they forced Simon of Cyrene to carry his cross. Jesus was so tired. He could hardly move, even after Simon took the cross. What was so remarkable to me is that he never said a mumbling word. I wished he would have said something.

They even took his robe and gambled with it. This was a very humiliating act. It was not enough to crucify him in public. This was humiliating enough by itself. They had to rub it in. It was like kicking someone once they were down.

I was also there when Jesus cried out, "My God, my God, why have you forsaken me?" At first I thought it was the cry of a forsaken man. But then his lips kept moving. But no words came out; his face all of a sudden had peace written all over it. It was as if the pain were gone and he was alone with God. I stopped feeling sorry for him then because I knew he was all right. He finally took his last breath and died.

Do not think it was over when Jesus died. All of a sudden the earth began to shake. Rocks began to split. You could hear cloth being ripped in the Temple. I did not find out until after the commotion that the veil that separated the Holy of Holies from ordinary people like me was split in two, allowing all of us to have access to God. Then the graves started opening up, and the saints from over the years began to come out of their graves. I recognized only a few, who were talked about in Scripture. Others recognized other saints. Earlier, some thought maybe Jesus was calling Elijah to come save him. Well, can you believe it? One of the saints looked like Elijah. When I saw all of this, I said to myself, "I have no more doubt; surely this is the Son of God." I knew then that Jesus was no pretender. He was no impostor. I saw the power of God at work despite the death of Jesus. Jesus was never alone. God was there all the time. God was there all the time. Yes, God was there all the time.

A Story About Praying for Those Who Hate You and Ridicule You

I was present in chapel at Garrett-Evangelical Theological Seminary in October, 1985, when President Neal Fisher retold

the following story. It is a story of how important it is to quote
Scripture or perform acts of prayer, following Jesus' example
on the cross. This story can be used to encourage people who
think things are hopeless and that God has deserted them.

> You have probably heard of Robert Coles and his work with
> the children of the poor during the Civil Rights struggle. He
> wrote a book called *Children of Bondage* in which he record-
> ed stories of how children had to face segregation and
> desegregation. He tells one story of a young African
> American girl who was being ushered to school by state mar-
> shals when desegregation was being ordered. She was the
> first person to integrate that particular school. People were
> standing around her shouting particularly harsh and nasty
> things. There were all kinds of people trying to humiliate
> and discourage her, including mothers holding babies in
> their arms. A reporter noted that this little girl was mum-
> bling inaudible words under her breath. Later that day the
> reporter asked the little girl what she had been mumbling
> about. She said, "I was praying for all those people who
> don't want me to go to school."

Let this mind be in you, which was also in Christ Jesus. Jesus
often handled ridicule and danger by reciting Scripture. While
on the cross, he prayed for his enemies. He said, "Father, forgive
them: for they know not what they do" (Luke 23:34). The paral-
lel between what Jesus said and what the little African American
girl said is striking.

God does not abandon us in life. God may be silent. God is,
however, always present. God is not an abusive parent. Rather,
God encourages us to express the negative feelings we have as a
means of moving toward wholeness.

PART TWO

JESUS' HANDLING
OF OTHERS' SHAME

In the first part of this book, attention was paid to how Jesus responded to shame-based situations and the implications that his response has for us. In part 2 we will shift from Jesus' handling of his own shame to how Jesus responded to shame-based situations that had the potential for shaming others. The focus of the mimetic implication has to do with treating ourselves the way Jesus responded to others. More precisely, the point is that our feelings about ourselves are based on the internalization of our relationships with others. Through the process of role identification we can insert ourselves into biblical characters and scenes and internalize what it is like to have Jesus respond to our shame. In other words, we can experience renewal by identification with and internalization of biblical scenes involving Jesus and thereby internalize Jesus' accepting attitude as part of ourselves.

Depth psychology, object relations theory, psychoanalytic theory, self psychology, and the psychology of shame all point to the fact that self-identity develops based on the quality of internalizations we take in from the significant others in the environment of our early lives. If these internalizations are positive and accepting, then we have internalized an enduring source of self-identity that can nourish and sustain us throughout our lives. Conversely, if our internalizations are punitive and frustrating, we have taken into ourselves sources for undermining and sabotaging our self-development. Such internalizations become continuous sources of shame. What part 2 suggests is that people with punitive and frustrating internalization can find sources for countering these negative internalizations through the internalization of biblical scenes in which Jesus is actively transforming the shame of someone he encountered. The stories in which Jesus encounters shame-based people and transforms their shame into positive self-affirmation can be retold from the pulpit and in pastoral counseling. Such retelling of Jesus' activities, along with contemporary stories, can become a transforming source that can counter the shame scenes that the shame-based person internalized early in her or his life.

CHAPTER FOUR

SUCH A FAITH
I HAVE NOT SEEN

"I tell you, not even in Israel have I found such faith."
(LUKE 7:9 NRSV)

In Luke 7:1-10 and Matthew 8:5-13, we have the story of Jesus healing the centurion's servant. Crossan says that Jesus' healing events and table arrangement scenes point to Jesus' attempt to address indirectly the shame-and-honor-based culture of his day. I think that the story of healing the centurion's servant is precisely one of those stories that fit neatly into Crossan's observation. In this story Jesus did not care that the centurion was not part of his religious group, nor was he intimidated by the laws governing relationships that Jews had with non-Jews. Jesus would not allow the centurion's Gentile group identity to prevent him from extending healing and grace to one of God's children.

Many people come to church and to pastoral counseling with the same self-attitude as the centurion. He believed that he was not worthy to have Jesus associate with him. He would not think of Jesus ever coming to his house. Luke's account, more than Matthew's, gives us some clues as to why the centurion might have felt unworthy. Jesus responded to the centurion in Luke and Matthew in a way that did not make the centurion's non-Jewish status a barrier to relating to the man. God's grace and healing were extended by Jesus without regard to social status.

The concern of this chapter is to explore how Jesus related to people who were considered to be of less value than others because of their non-Jewish group membership or because of their being deemed unworthy or unclean because of certain behaviors they exhibited.

THE HEALING OF THE CENTURION'S SERVANT

John Meier argues that Jesus' healing stories were authentic aspects of his historical ministry.[1]

> To summarize: various criteria of historicity suggest that the historical Jesus performed certain actions during his public ministry that both he and some of his contemporaries thought were miraculous healing of the sick or infirm. Major types of such healings involved persons suffering from various skin ailments (leprosy) and persons who were deaf and/or mute.[2]

My own concern is to establish the point that Jesus' healings were occasions when his honor and shame were severely challenged in an indirect way and when Jesus consciously decided not to let his ministry be governed by the in-group and out-group values of his contemporary society and religion. The healing of the centurion's servant is a good example of an encounter of Jesus with his culture and religious tradition. He truly was inaugurating a new world, one that was egalitarian and functioned by different rules.

The following is what we know about the centurion and Jesus' encounter with him. The centurion was a Gentile, or non-Jew. He was commanding officer of a group of soldiers; the unit commanded by officers of the centurion ranks was the backbone of the Roman army.[3] Centurion was the highest rank to which an ordinary soldier could aspire. The job included disciplining soldiers; supervising the government's execution of criminals (crucifixions); overseeing drills; and supervising armaments, headquarters, and company and field commands. Centurions were paid by the government and were in charge of public order.

In Luke's account, the centurion is described as the first Gentile to encounter Jesus and one who was well respected by Jesus. The venue of the healing of the servant was in Capernaum where there were toll stations for travelers and a military garrison.

The centurion's Gentile heritage is emphasized by Luke and Matthew, which means that the story likely has a common source.[4] For a Jew like Jesus to enter into the house of a Gentile meant, according to the Jewish religious tradition, that the Jew would be defiled. Defilement meant becoming ritually unclean. Luke particularly highlights the fact that the centurion knew of these social conventions and deemed himself unworthy to have Jesus come into his home. The centurion knew of Jesus' reputation and did not believe that Jesus had to risk violating the religious laws of defilement in order for his servant to be healed.

Luke pictures the centurion as sending a Jewish party to entreat Jesus to heal the servant. Luke's account has Jesus deciding to go where the servant was and not being intimidated by the laws of defilement. The centurion, however, convinced of his unworthiness, sent a second Jewish party to Jesus indicating that there was no real need for Jesus to come. His rationale was that Jesus only needed to say the word and his servant would be healed, even from a long distance. Luke portrays Jesus as being moved by the centurion's faith and healing the servant without coming in contact with the centurion.

Of particular note are the words that Jesus says in Luke 7:9. He says he had not seen such faith in Israel. For me this highlights the fact that in every situation in which Jesus exercised his ministry, there was a potential risk for his rejection and humiliation. He seemed to be saying these words for the benefit of those in the religious in-group who were rejecting his message. Norman Perrin, in his book *Rediscovering the Teachings of Jesus,* includes the criterion of religious conflict with religious officials as a means of establishing the historicity of Jesus' authentic sayings.[5] The potential for the rejection and humiliation of Jesus in this setting could be another criterion for the authenticity of the accounts of Jesus' healing stories.

The major point to be made about this encounter of Jesus with the centurion is that Jesus refused to allow the religious laws against defilement to stand in the way of his healing activity. Such laws were the basis of an honor and shame hierarchy in which some were deemed clean and others unclean. Such practices affected the self-evaluation of those deemed unclean very negatively. Jesus sought a different means by which society could evaluate people.

THE CENTURION'S SHAME

In this section I want to explore Michael Lewis's attributional view of shame as a way to explore the centurion's shame and how

Jesus responded to it. I also want to combine Gershen Kaufman's view on the cultural triggers of shame with Lewis's attributional theory of shame to highlight Jesus' sensitivity to shame issues.

The attributional theory of shame finds its orientation in determining whether shame is internal, external, specific, or global.[6] Attribution refers to how individuals interpret potentially shameful and guilt producing situations. Internal shame is the internalization of shame so that the sources of shame are attributed to be from within. External shame means that the person does not take the shame into the self. Global shame means that the shame is attributed to the total self, whereas specific shame is only attributed to one's behavior. In Lewis's view, shame results from the internalization of global shame such that the cause of the shame is attributed to be from within, and guilt is the result of the specific attribution of blame to one's behavior and not the self.

It is clear that the centurion felt shame. It is also apparent that he was aware of the Jewish taboo against entering the house of a Gentile. Whether the centurion actually internalized this negative attitude about being unclean is speculative. For example, he had close association with Jews, for the centurion had built their synagogue (Luke 7:5). Moreover, Jews saw him as an acceptable Gentile. Perhaps his acceptance was based on his own rejection of his Gentile heritage. This would lessen people's awareness of his unclean status. Such rejection of one's own heritage is called self-hatred. This is plausible, although not provable, given the data.

Of significance is the fact that the centurion did not want Jesus to violate the defilement taboo. This is further validation that the centurion could have internalized the negative attitudes of the dominant in-group. That is, he made himself acceptable to others by defacing himself in order to be acceptable to those in the in-group. His goal seemed to be to make others as comfortable as possible by not calling attention to his non-Jewish heritage. He survived by not challenging the social status quo. He never risked rejection by asking Jews to violate their cleanliness code of conduct. He did not attempt to find out whether Jesus would transcend the current social conventions in order to care for him or his servant.

In Luke's account, however, Jesus made the decision to violate the code. Jesus made up his mind immediately that the health of the centurion's servant was more important than maintaining the cleanliness code. The centurion, however, insisted that Jesus not violate the code, and Jesus finally relented and healed the servant from a distance.

Gershen Kaufman's theory of how shame is triggered in people is of significance in understanding the centurion's behavior. In Kaufman's view, culture activates shame as much as families and peers do.[7] Each culture has rules for predicting, controlling, and responding to experiences. These rules carry with them systems of evaluating people and are powerful forces of social control. Certain groups have negative images attached to them, and the internalization of these negative images by group members can lead to shame. Thus, avoiding those situations that can trigger these negative images of shame is important. The centurion seemed to be attempting to avoid such feelings.

The key to understanding the behavior of Jesus and the centurion with regard to negative images of shame has to do with the need of the centurion's servant. Although the potential existed for Jesus to make an indirect political statement about a shamed-based culture, both Jesus and the centurion decided that it was not time to make such a statement. The centurion felt that the servant's health was more important, and Jesus reluctantly agreed.

MIMETIC IMPLICATIONS

Jesus' willingness to risk defilement and encounter the wrath of his religious community by entering the centurion's home needs further comment. We need to internalize the accepting attitude that Jesus had toward the centurion so that we can see the way Jesus saw the centurion. Jesus was able to respond from a distance to the centurion's deeply held self-devaluation and was willing to go to great lengths to affirm the centurion. Those of us who carry shame need to learn to respond to ourselves the way Jesus responded to the centurion.

According to Kaufman's model, shame is the internalization of negative governing scenes occurring early in life. Shame is also the global attributing of worthlessness to oneself, in Lewis's model. Although shame can be activated by negative cultural images, the sources of devaluation are internalized in both models. This does not mean that one's shame is only in the mind. Rather, actual shaming events have taken place; however, the person responds to shaming events in ways that completely undermine positive self-esteem.

To overcome negative governing scenes and pejorative global attributions, it is necessary to internalize positive scenes, experiences, and significant others. Kaufman emphasizes the need for "reparative, security-giving relationships" that heal by providing new opportunities for positive identifications.[8] New relationships, as well as opportunities for new images for reinterpreting the original governing scenes and negative attributions, are needed, according to Kaufman.[9] Such a process of internalization is cognitive and conscious, involving metaphors and stories that can actually reshape the internalized governing scene. For Kaufman, therapy is developing a new language that transforms one's inner life.[10]

The recognition that it is possible to heal one's inner life through new relationships and the use of metaphors and stories makes preaching and pastoral counseling very important. It is possible to retell the stories of Jesus in ways that allow people to internalize the scenes where Jesus responds to the shame of those he encounters.

It must be added that preaching by itself cannot completely do the job of helping people internalize new and more positive scenes. Preaching, pastoral counseling, and new relationships are viewed as holistic entities that must work together in order for the shame-based person to derive the best healing. Preaching can initiate the process of reinternalization and can also augment the process of healing. Preaching, however, needs to be accompanied by other relationships, such as pastoral counseling and supportive small groups.

It is in the internalization of biblical scenes of Jesus that we find the ability to transform the earlier negative governing scenes of shame. The shame-based person identifies with the roles of the one who was shamed as well as with Jesus, who accepts the shame-prone person.[11] The person also identifies with the plot of the story, which raises the expectation that her or his life will follow a similar pattern and eventuate in a comparable outcome.

When new scenes are internalized and when new and more accepting relationships are taken into the self, positive attributions toward the self begin to emerge and more nurturing self-images take the place of the old, punitive self-images and attributions. Slowly, a new self begins to emerge, one that is more self-accepting and confident.

RETELLING THE STORY

Let us retell the story of the centurion from his point of view. He will be the narrator of the story, and the focus will be on his internal process of handling Jesus' positive attitude toward him. The contemporary story will be about a woman whose shame was activated by recalling an earlier and central scene of shame and how her identification with the story of the centurion pleading the case of the sick servant gave her hope that Jesus was coming to heal her.

The method of retelling the story of how Jesus related to the centurion's shame needs to proceed in such a way that the contemporary counselee or parishioner is compelled to identify with the centurion. Without coercion, of course, the rhetorical power of the retelling needs to invite the hearer to identify based on the similarity between the hearer's and the centurion's shame. Also, the retelling needs to make perfectly clear that Jesus was determined that nothing, especially societal norms of shame and honor, would stand in the way of his ministry to someone in need. The hearer needs to be convinced that shame, even that activated by cultural and religious images of failure and defilement current in Jesus' day, is not a barrier that will prevent the healing ministry of Jesus.

The Centurion's Story

I am really concerned about my employee. He has been sick now for some time, and nothing that we do seems to work. If something is not done soon, my employee will die.

Throughout Capernaum, village people have been talking about the Jewish healer named Jesus. It seems as if he has been spending a considerable amount of time here and considers Capernaum his home. They say this man not only performs the miracle of healing, he also extends his concern for people's well-being beyond his own religious group and friends. His healing reputation includes non-Jews as well. This must be some fantastic person who would risk the wrath of his own religious colleagues to care for the needs of others regardless of their religious affiliation.

I know Jesus will heal my employee if I ask him. There is no doubt in my mind. In my spirit I feel compelled to pursue this possibility. I also know the political reality of the laws of social defilement and cleanliness, and there is no way that I would want to put Jesus in an awkward position where he would have to violate rules. I know he would violate the religious rules for me, but I am not worth the risk. I would never allow Jesus to come into my home and be contaminated by me. This would make me feel so terrible, and I would never forgive myself.

I have made up my mind. I will not approach Jesus myself. I will talk to some of my Jewish friends. I am thinking of those for whom I have just built a synagogue. This way Jesus will not be put in a difficult situation. They will intercede for me, and a bad situation will be avoided.

As expected, my Jewish friends did not let me down. They told me what they said to Jesus. They told him that I had an employee who was seriously ill and in need of healing. They said that Jesus never hesitated. He decided that he would come to see my employee, who was staying at my home. "Oh, no!" I thought. "He must not come here. This would certainly mean that he would get into trouble with his own people. I cannot let this happen."

I asked my Jewish friends to leave immediately and stop Jesus before he got to my home. I asked them to tell him to heal my employee from a distance. Certainly, he could do this and not expose himself to controversy on my behalf. When they returned, they said that Jesus reluctantly consented, and when I went to my employee's room, he was healed.

I will never forget the fact that Jesus wanted to risk public embarrassment for me. He is an amazing person. He insisted on treating me as somebody. He saw me as a person of worth. Truly, he is the son of God.

A Contemporary Story

In my counseling experiences over the years, I have seen several people who believed that they were absolutely worthless and unlovable. They felt that their behavior was so despicable that God could not possibly care for them and that they would be severely judged for their behavior. What struck me about these people was that their shame was totally consuming, far beyond a healthy shame that could be relieved by confession. Their shame was about their very existence. There was very little I could do to persuade them or help change their minds about their conviction of worthlessness.

I am thinking of one person who felt her sins were so unforgivable that she could not even approach God in prayer. She could not call God's name without anxiety. It took over two years of counseling before she would allow herself to entertain the possibility that God might not be as rejecting of her as she felt.

It has been my experience in pastoral counseling that people with shame—believing they are flawed and unlovable—need considerable time in caring relationships before they are able to respond to any idea that God might care for them. Devastating shame blocks people's ability to discern a caring God. They need to spend time in a mediating relationship with some caring others before they can entertain the notion that God or Jesus could actually care about them. In this particular case it was at least two years before her shame was sufficiently neutralized so she could discuss God or Jesus in relationship to herself.

The change came one day when I least expected it. At every chance that presented itself, I would remind her of some Bible story in which Jesus did not act according to the expected pattern of condemnation she expected. She would not allow herself to believe that Jesus would act in any other way than to condemn. One day she made reference to something she inadvertently heard on the radio. She heard a minister say that God could forgive anything if God forgave David. She was brought up in the church and remembered the stories of David and Moses. She had in her mind that God did *not* forgive David or

Moses for their sins. She then said, "If God will not forgive his chosen, what makes you think God can forgive me?" My response was that I was glad she was finally allowing herself to talk about her relationship with God. I asked her if she were ready to explore her relationship with God, a subject that had given her so much anxiety in the past. She said she was. I, therefore, asked her to reread the story of David and his relationship with Bathsheba in 2 Samuel 11–12. She was very aware of the story of how he took another man's wife and had sexual intercourse with her and how the prophet Nathan confronted David with the sin. She was also aware that a child was born from the sin of David and the child died. She interpreted the death of the child as David's punishment. She also believed that God would punish her by harming her children. This story of David frightened her, and she believed that God would punish her by striking down one or more of her children. What a terrible threat it was to live under that kind of belief! She was emotionally tormented, and her shame would not let her escape.

My suggestion was that she read again this story about David, and then turn to Psalm 51 and read it. I told her we could discuss it in a later counseling session if she desired. The very next week she came back and wanted to know the connection between David and Psalm 51. I mentioned that this was a psalm that many believe referred to David and his encounter with Nathan. She said she figured as much. What happened next was very interesting. She began to talk about her dead father who she said had always been her guardian angel and her voice of conscience over the years. She said her father would always be a guide for her through his spirit and would never steer her in the wrong direction. She said that her life would go in the right direction whenever she listened to the voice of her dead father speaking through her conscience.

She began to consciously link her dad with God's presence in her life. Although she felt she had a destructive bent in her life, she began to see that the voice of her father never failed to warn her about trouble she was getting into. She began to see a connection between behaving in self-destructive ways and her continued shame. She began to see that God was not trying to punish her, but was trying to help her to find God's forgiveness in the same way that David found God's forgiveness. This awareness that God cared for her all along, through the voice of her dead father, made all the difference in the world to her shame being transformed.

CONCLUSION

These stories can be used in preaching and pastoral counseling by telling them from the point of view of the one who carries the shame. The story needs to be told in ways that help the hearer to identify and sympathize with the shame-based person in the story. Once the shame of the person is told, the preacher or counselor needs to introduce the transforming aspects of the story so that the hearer can have firmly planted in his or her mind new possibilities for dealing with his or her shame. The key to telling the story is to make sure that the alternative to shame is told in a dramatic way, so that the hearer can see the point of new self-expectations.

CHAPTER FIVE

SHAME
AND CONFESSION

"Therefore I tell you, her sins, which are many, are forgiven, for she loved much; but he who is forgiven little, loves little."

In the story of the woman anointing Jesus' feet with her tears and precious ointment in Luke 7, we have an excellent example of how Jesus graciously and sensitively responded to another person's shame. In this case it was a woman whose self-invitation to the house of another helped to set the scene in which Jesus responded graciously to another's shame. Jesus was very gentle, tender, and caring—in contrast to the host.

The host in the story is a man whose role was to call attention to the local, conventional shame wisdom. This man thought in categories of shame or cultural precipitants of shame. According to Kaufman, one cultural precipitant of shame is class distinction.[1] The host placed people into class categories and treated them differently based on their category.[2] The host saw the woman as a sinner or as one with whom a truly holy man would not associate. Jesus, however, functioning according to an eschatological vision of the dawning of a new community based on unconventional wisdom, did not hesitate in relating closely with the woman.

The behavior of the woman, though not according to the appropriate protocol of that day, can be viewed as a confession of her shame. Her tears, her anointing of Jesus' feet, and Jesus' parable of the response of the one forgiven, all point to the fact that the behavior of the woman can be seen as a confession of her sins. Jesus interpreted her bold approach to him as a confession and extended absolution to her through the words: "Thy sins are forgiven" (Luke 7:48).

This woman's assertive behavior in inviting herself to the food table is related to the potential of having her shame relieved. The host, however, doubted Jesus' status when he thought to himself, "If this man were a prophet, he would have known who and what sort of woman this is who is touching him, for she is a sinner" (Luke 7:39 RSV). The attitude of the host conveys the conventional wisdom of the religious community, but it also sets the stage for showing how Jesus went against the thinking of his day. According to contemporary Jesus scholars, Jesus often chose the food table as a place to show the contrast between the nonshame egalitarian kingdom of God and the shame-based value system of society.[3]

Just as in other chapters, this chapter will explore this event— Jesus at the host's house and the woman anointing his feet—from the standpoint of contemporary shame theory and contemporary New Testament scholarship in order to set the stage for telling stories. I will further explore the confession of shame as a psychological means of lessening its impact, as well as provide commentary on the role of table association in Jesus' ministry.

A SHAME THEORY OF CONFESSION

Psychologically, confessing shame or guilt is an attempt to acknowledge that shame has occurred and to relieve it by going to others and telling them about it.[4] The difference between shame and guilt is that shame involves global attributions of fault to the entire self while guilt is attributed to a specific act.[5] Since the sin of the uninvited woman is not spelled out, it can be assumed that no specific act is involved. Therefore, she is dealing with a feeling that her entire self is shameful. In the process of confessing shame, one externalizes the shame.[6] That is, shame is acknowledged by allowing oneself to be aware of its existence, but one detaches the self from it by means of placing it outside the self. This is a way of observing one's shame, in an objective way, apart from the self. Here the externalization enables one to move from being the observed to the observer. Confession is also a way of undoing the original shame scene. In the original shame, some expectation or standard was not met, and the person attributed blame and fault to the entire self, not just to the behavior.

In the case in Luke 7, the woman's inappropriate approach to Jesus and her aggressive behavior as an uninvited guest were motivated by a need to confess. Contemporary shame theory sheds light on the assertive behavior of the woman. There is within us a need to confess our transgression through the reenactment of our original shame. For example, Michael Lewis points out that confessing to a person of status is very similar to reenacting an original scene of shame in which the shame was generated within a parent-child relationship.[7] Just as the original shaming event may have taken place in the presence of a parental figure or some adult in authority, the reversing of the shame also comes when the shaming is undone in the presence of a parent figure or someone who has authority. In other words, confession takes on added meaning when done in the presence of a person who is endowed with authority and status. Thus, to confess, in shame theory, is to reenact in a positive way the original shame scene in which the parent was the authority. This confession helps to undo the shame when forgiveness is pronounced by the parent figure.

It is very obvious that Jesus was a person of such stature. The host appears to have extended the eating invitation to Jesus, knowing by his reputation his status as a healer and teacher. The entire story represents the fact that Jesus had the authority and stature to hear confessions and to pronounce absolution.

THE POTENTIAL RIDICULE OF JESUS

Earlier I suggested that one of the criterion for knowing whether a particular saying or scene of Jesus is authentic is the criterion of the potential for the humiliation of Jesus. Here was an opportunity for the embarrassment of Jesus. Obviously the religious host sought in every way to humiliate Jesus. He provided no water to wash Jesus' feet, which was contrary to customary hospitality. He did not greet Jesus at all. It looks as if Jesus came into a hostile situation where he could be closely scrutinized.

Jesus was not oblivious to the potentially embarrassing setup. In fact, he called it to the attention of the host when the host looked disparagingly at Jesus' care for the woman. Such a setting was typical for Jesus. One way to resist the changes that Jesus was bringing about was to try to ridicule him and embarrass him at every occasion, in order to show the public that he was not the person they thought he was.

Rather than being humiliated, Jesus used such an occasion to teach about the nature of God's reign. Contemporary scholarship on Jesus' table associations has highlighted how Jesus sought to demonstrate the contrast between the honor-and-shame-ordered society and the nonshame, egalitarian rule of God that he was inaugurating. Crossan comments on table associations using the concept of commensality. For Crossan, commensality refers to nondiscriminating table associations that clashed fundamentally with the honor and shame values of the ancient Mediterranean culture.[8]

> The idea of eating together and living together without any distinctions, differentness, discriminations, or hierarchies is close to the irrational and the absurd. And the one who advocates or does it is close to the deviant and the perverted. He has no honor. He has no shame.[9]

Table associations in Jesus' day were not mere eating events. They were economic happenings that marked rules of distinction. They represented a map of class and economic distinction, a social hierarchy, and political differentiation.[10] What Jesus was doing, then, represented open commensality in which no distinctions were made on the basis of honor or shame. He was advocating a form of radical egalitarianism.

By allowing the woman to anoint him with her hair and ointment, Jesus was demonstrating what the new world would be like. His parable of forgiveness and grace was a way to teach the host about the true hospitality of the reign of God. Although the dominant interpretation of the passage has been related to Jesus and his being anointed as a sign of being a messiah, understanding shame and honor and how it worked in Jesus' society allows a different interpretation, one that takes into account how Jesus related to those who where shamed.

According to Marcus J. Borg, not only did Jesus' open commensality violate conventional wisdom regarding table associations, it also violated conventional wisdom regarding how men related to women.[11] First, Jesus' behavior with regard to women was radical in that he paid very little attention to patriarchal values. There were rigid boundaries separating women from men in Jesus' time. Women were not regarded as the social equals of men, and therefore they were not welcome in male company. They sat in sections in the synagogue separated from men and were not counted in making a quorum for holding a prayer meeting.

Second, any respected Jewish man would never talk to a woman in public. Part of this had to do with the insecurity about the sexual boundaries between males and females.[12] Temptation needed to be avoided at all costs.

Third, Jesus' behavior when associating with women was continually consistent and would have been considered shocking and inappropriate in his day. It was very unusual to see a gender mixed group traveling together. "The sight of a sexually mixed group traveling with a Jewish holy man must have been provocative."[13] Some contemporary scholars have questioned Jesus' commitment to celibacy and conjectured that Jesus must have been married.[14]

My own point of view is that Jesus' behavior with regard to associating with women, even in situations of emotional closeness and intimacy, was completely consistent with his views on open commensality and radical egalitarianism. His behavior reflected his commitment to the coming reign of God, rooted in a nonshame system. Moreover, Jesus' ability to handle himself appropriately in close proximity with women speaks to the importance of creating a safe environment so that women could feel free to approach him with their shame. Today we recognize the significance and importance of maintaining sexual boundaries when trying to undo the shame that people have.[15] I would suggest that Jesus was aware of this need to maintain secure boundaries in his relating to women and men. To suggest otherwise would be an attempt to totally discredit the relevance of the historical Jesus. The fact that there is no record of Jesus misusing his position to gain sexual favors from women points not only to his awareness of his ultimate mission but also to his understanding of the nature of shame. People need to expose their true vulnerability and shame without fear of being exploited. Only in safe and secure relationships, in which the threat of exploitation of vulnerability is at a minimum, can the legacy of shame be undone.

MIMETIC IMPLICATIONS

It is possible to tell stories of Jesus' relating to the shame of others in ways that people can internalize new scenes in order to counteract the old shaming scenes. This is possible because people can internalize the entire scene and the roles of the different characters in the story. Stories, such as the one of the woman anointing Jesus' feet, told in loving and caring relationships and in preaching and in pastoral counseling, can do much to assist people in changing the damage done by original shame scenes and replacing them with more positive scenes. Below is the retelling of the biblical story of the woman's anointing and a contemporary story that represents some of the insights generated in the above discussion.

RETELLING THE ANCIENT STORY

The goal of retelling the story of the woman anointing Jesus' feet is to make the story an invitation to the hearer to internalize the entire scene of Jesus' encounter with the woman for the purposes of enabling the shame-based hearer to come to grips with his or her shame. To this end, it is important to introduce the characters in the scene very carefully.[16] The needs of the shame-based woman anointing Jesus' feet have to be made clear, and the contrast in the behavior of the original host and Jesus' behavior needs to also be spelled out.

In the days that Jesus walked the earth the protocol surrounding eating and table associations was extremely important. Sanctions for and against associating with in-group and out-group members were clear and strictly enforced. Association with certain people, particularly those regarded as sinners, would contaminate the entire gathering of people. Religious leaders, especially, were never to associate with the wrong people.

Jesus was invited to eat in the home of a noted religious leader of that day. Jesus accepted the invitation. Upon entering the home, he discovered that there was a woman present who was considered to be a sinner by religious standards. Although her sins were not mentioned, she was considered to be an untouchable. It was clear that she was not an invited guest. She had crashed the dinner party. She had two things against her. She was a sinner, and she was a female.

The woman could be viewed as a bold and assertive uninvited guest, yet the woman was not expelled from the dinner. She was allowed to approach Jesus and to anoint his feet with her tears and oil. By today's standards, to be unwanted and not invited and then to wash someone else's feet would be considered an act of self-hatred and self-denigration. To us, her behavior was nauseating, and to be aware of gender meant that this woman would need to come to grips with her blind adherence to patriarchy. It must be made clear here that Jesus was already behaving in a revolutionary way with regard to women by being in their company. Jesus also seemed to be aware of the woman's need and her feelings of shame. He believed that relating to the woman was more important than the religious rules against associating with women.

It is obvious that the woman needed to respond to Jesus in the way that she did. She was motivated by something very powerful in her life. The clue to her motivation came from Jesus himself, who made her motives clear in the parable he told to the original host. The parable was about the response that people give to being forgiven of their sins. It was clear to Jesus that this woman was very thankful for Jesus' forgiving presence.

But, you might ask, when did Jesus actually forgive this woman? When did the transaction of forgiveness actually occur between Jesus and the woman? Forgiveness does not appear to be by formula. It appears to be through a process of interaction between Jesus and the woman. It was in Jesus' gracious approachability and acceptance of the woman that she felt forgiven. Jesus' whole personhood communicated to the woman that she was accepted—despite her past sins.

The scene shifts to the religious leader who had condemned Jesus and the woman. The religious leader helped to give added significance to what Jesus did. Obviously, the expectations of the religious man were a reminder to Jesus of the religious standards of the day and that Jesus was violating them.

The inhospitable host's behavior was typical for a religious leader of that day and contrasted sharply with Jesus' behavior and the behavior of the woman. Not only was Jesus not really wanted at the dinner, neither was the woman. Jesus was provided no water for his tired feet, which hosts customarily offered guests who had walked some distances. More important, the status of the woman changed in the story, from that of a guest to a host, by the way she responded to Jesus. Jesus' behavior embraced the woman and allowed her to expose her shame in his presence. The exchange between Jesus and the woman was very intimate, and it is obvious that the original host was very uncomfortable with what he was witnessing. The way the woman handled herself in Jesus' presence was thought by some to resemble the kind of relationship a woman would have with her husband, since she exposed her hair in the way she did. Yet, Jesus was not uncomfortable with the woman's behavior, nor was the woman fearful of having her vulnerability exploited. What she was doing was presenting her whole self to Jesus, flaws and all, and Jesus did not let her down. He communicated to her the hospitality and care she needed to come to grips with her shame.

A CONTEMPORARY STORY

As a Ph.D. candidate at Boston University, I witnessed how a colleague responded to the shame of a man with disarming openness and graciousness. The story of Jesus relating to the uninvited guest reminded me of this story.

My colleague and I worked together at the Solomon Carter Fuller Mental Health Center at Boston University. The center is named after the first African American psychiatrist to finish Boston University Medical School. Our offices were housed in a three-story tenement house owned by Springfield Baptist Church in the South End of Boston.

One day a young African American adult male came through the door of the building housing our offices. He was poor, wore disheveled clothing, and at times appeared to be very aggressive and belligerent. He would not leave. Frankly, he was a nuisance and got on my nerves. Everyone was uncomfortable with him being around and tried to find ways for him to leave. I tried my hand in getting him to leave, and he refused. He reminded me of present day aggressive panhandlers who are homeless. I threatened him with calling the police; he looked at me as if to say "go right ahead." I did not handle the scene appropriately, and I had to give up. I had no clue about the man's need, and I had to allow someone else to try to respond to him. He and I did not connect at all.

My colleague, who was Caucasian and a senior member of the staff, intervened. His goal, in contrast to my goal, was to build a relationship with the man. Almost immediately, the man responded positively. My colleague attended to the man in a way that won the man's confidence. After about an hour with the man, my colleague was able to take the man over to the psychiatric ward of the hospital with the man's blessing. Apparently the man was frequently in and out of mental institutions and required special treatment, and my colleague, with much more experience than I, realized this.

What I learned from how my colleague related to the man has always stayed with me. I learned how to relate to people who are exhibiting bizarre and inappropriate behavior. I learned how to make myself available to them and to build a relationship in order to find out what their needs are. The man was obviously looking for a friendly face and a caring environment. He thought he could find it in our center. When he found it, he was able to express his need. He needed help in securing more medication for his mental illness.

One more incident happened with this man that reminds me of the story of the invited guest. While we were in the waiting room of the psychiatric ward, the man did something to show his gratitude to my friend. He got down on his hands and knees and tried to kiss the feet of my colleague. Gently, my colleague prevented him from doing so and said in a caring way, "your words of thanks are enough."

As a young African American male, I was looking at the man in need through the cultural eyes of shame. I saw him as an interruption of my busy schedule. I saw him as a nuisance and not as a person. I was like the religious leader in the story of the uninvited woman. I condemned the man because he did not have the same values as I and because society would look down on him. My colleague, however, responded to him as to a unique person and not a stereotype of a homeless person, and the man was grateful to him. The man then expressed his gratitude in the way he could. The man responded to the genuineness of my colleague and felt good about him. My colleague was able to look beyond his faults and see his needs.

In both stories, the shame-based values of the culture were prominent. They influenced the care that was delivered. People in counseling or in our churches may bring similar shame to church or to counseling, looking for a word from the Lord. The failures for which people feel ashamed are numerous, and people need to know that they will not be condemned for them. Telling the stories of Jesus, as well as contemporary stories, can help people internalize stories that may help them fight deeply ingrained feelings of shame and nonacceptance. They can reenact the scenes in ways that change their belief and convictions about themselves.

CONCLUSION

The emphasis in using these two stories in pastoral counseling should be on the safety and security that is needed for confessing one's shame. I have told these stories in counseling to help those who have never had a safe place to confess their shame to know that counseling is a safe place where they do not have to fear being exploited. I also have used the stories to help people discuss their reluctance to express their shame in the counseling process.

In preaching I have used these stories to help create the expectation that there are safe places where one's shame can be expressed and healed. In addition, I have emphasized that in the role of caring for others, we must help create a safe environment where others can express their shame without the fear of having their shame misused.

CHAPTER SIX

COME OUT,
YOU UNCLEAN SPIRIT

For he had said to him, "Come out of the man, you unclean spirit!"
(MARK 5:8 RSV; SEE MARK 5:1-20; MATTHEW 8:28-34; AND LUKE 8:26-39)

A key element in a conviction about one's shame is being excluded from communities because of fear that others might be threatened. Such fears have fueled many tragic events in human history, particularly the fear of those who had incurable diseases, had mental illness, or were demon possessed. People with these ailments were and are banished from communities by those who feel threatened. People with fear tend to want to eliminate from their presence and community anything they do not comprehend or cannot control.

One of the activators of shame in people who have the above ailments is exclusion from community. Such exclusion breaks the interpersonal bridge that people need in order to feel loved and accepted. To be excluded affirms one's unacceptableness and sets in motion a series of shame-based self-convictions.

In this chapter I will examine how Jesus responded to the shame of a demon possessed person. The goal is to help people who feel excluded from community because of their peculiar and frightening behavior to internalize stories of Jesus as a means of countering negative, shame-based, internalized stories and scenes about themselves.

MY INITIAL INTEREST IN THE GERASENE DEMONIAC

My first encounter with the story of the Gerasene demoniac was when I was a child. I heard my father tell this poor, unfortunate man's story. My father's emphasis was not on the first part of the story as recorded in Mark, however. Rather, his emphasis seemed to focus on the final scene of the story, in which the townspeople were frightened at what Jesus had done. In Mark 5:17-20, Jesus had boarded the boat in order to leave, and the formerly possessed man asked if he could accompany Jesus on his trip. Jesus told him no and that he needed to return home to spread the news about what had been done in his life. In other words, he was given a preaching assignment to declare and demonstrate what God had done in him through Jesus.

For my father the final scene was the crown and glory of the story because this man, who had once been alienated from community and lived among the graveyards and the tombs with dead people, was now alive and in his right mind. He was given permission from Jesus to return to the community from which he was excluded. Jesus did not want this man to run away from that community, according to my father; rather, Jesus wanted him to rejoin his original community, knowing that he would be a constant reminder of the power of God. He was in his right mind, and what was incomprehensible to them was now no longer a threat. The man was no longer wild or unruly. The basis of his exclusion and shame was no longer present.

My father would use his creative imagination when talking about the demoniac's return home. He would talk about the demoniac's return to his wife and children. He would say that on ordinary days the family members went about their normal daily routine. Then, the routine of the day would be disturbed when one of the demoniac's youngest children would spot his father coming, off at a distance. When the youngster spotted his father, he took the disturbing news to his mother. Knowing how abusive and destructive her husband was when he came home, she would instruct the family members to prepare the house like a fort to prevent their father's entrance. They were told to be quick about their protective activity if they were to avoid being terrorized or abused. Then, they began their activity of fortifying the home against their father.

My father would say that one day the youngster, who saw his father first, reported the approach of the father. But the boy also reported to the family that he was not sure that this was his father at all. The family members asked him why he thought this way.

The youngster pointed out that his father used to have a raging look in his eyes, but this man's face was no longer raging. His eyes and face looked peaceful and serene. He also said that the father usually had a frightening walk that was jerky, with sudden moves. But the youngster reported that now his father was walking steadily with no sudden moves. He also said that his father used to talk to himself in incoherent ways. But now, he said, this man must not be his father, because he was walking along humming an interesting tune. Hearing what the youngster was saying, they all ran to see what he was observing. They all confirmed that it was their father, and the wife's husband, but that he was in his right mind. My father said that the family stopped their protective behavior and their fortifying activity and left the house immediately to meet this renewed father and husband. A man who was once demon possessed was now in his right mind. They wanted to welcome him home and find out what happened to change his life.

This story has remained with me all my life. When I began to try to understand the phenomenon of shame and demon possession, I thought of the context in which my father told this story. It was through this narrative lens that I began to understand the relationship among shame, demon possession, and the process of excluding people whom we do not understand from community. Of course, in the case of abuse and the terror of those who are a threat to community, there needs to be an exclusion. The exclusion, however, still activates shame.

SCHOLARSHIP ON SHAME AND DEMON POSSESSION

John Dominic Crossan attempts to understand the demon possession reported in Mark 5 in light of the first-century mind. Drawing on anthropological studies of spirit possession and Shamanism, he says that there is a connection between demonic possession and colonial oppression.[1] The Gerasene demoniac seems to be an archtypal, or common, example of many cases of demon possession.[2] Among the social-psychological conclusions of many studies from cross-cultural and transtemporal perspectives is this: the context of demon possession seems to be (1) class antagonisms rooted in economic exploitation, (2) the eroding of long-standing traditions, and (3) colonial domination and revolution against it.[3] It seems that colonial domination and oppression produced a split in the personality of people with mental illness. It also appears that demon possession and mental illness took on the form of subtle protest against domination and were attempts at escaping oppression. According to this social psychological theory, demon possession was a form of coping with social and political oppression through deviant behavior.[4] For Crossan, demon possession is symbolic of attempts of individuals to revolt against oppression.[5]

Crossan's cross-cultural anthropological conclusions linking demon possession and oppression are plausible given contemporary theological and social psychological studies of oppressive cult activity. Some authors have observed that there is a relationship between demon possession and cultic ritual abuse in today's society.

First, there is a link between contemporary occult explosions and the phenomenon of demon possession.[6] Studies link contemporary interest in Satanism and cult activity to changes in Western civilization, including the weakening of established order, traditions, and religious commitment.[7] The same forces of social anomie, disorder, and meaninglessness gave rise to Nazism in Germany, which was an occult riddled society.

Those who are most susceptible to occult activity are those who feel what we have called shame. Those who have shame-based personalities feel isolated, connectionless, hopeless, unlovable, and confused. They are looking for someone or some group that will affirm and confirm them. Satanic groups, urban gangs, and Nazi-type White supremacy groups recruit their membership from such people. They make shame-prone people feel as if they belong and are connected.[8] Often, such people do not fully realize what they are getting themselves into until they get themselves deeply entrenched in the group and cannot escape the bondage that accompanies joining such groups. Once in, they find themselves completely dominated and oppressed. They lose any sense of individuality and agency that they once had. Other forces seem to be at work in them that lead to very self-destructive and other-destructive behavior.

My own religious views about demon possession and exorcism have been influenced by the unpublished work of Samuel Southard of Fuller Theological Seminary.[9] He gives a theological rationale for the contemporary presence and phenomenon of demon possession: it is not possible to distinguish between mental illness and demon possession except in two ways. First, the characteristics of possession and mental illness are the same. In order to find out whether a person is mentally ill or demon possessed, one must ascertain whether the person had ever been involved in a satanic cult or whether his or her parents had been involved in one. Sometimes people in satanic cults go through ritualistic acts of dedicating themselves to Satan. In other cases, some people were dedicated to Satan as babies as part of ritualistic services. Southard says that if occult activity is present and people have had significant participation in such groups, then the possibility of possession exists. If there is no occult activity present, chances are the person is dealing with emotional and mental illness. In cases of past occult activity, services of exorcism as well as psychotherapy are indicated. However, satanic groups have a great deal of difficulty allowing their subjects to flee from their bondage.

Second, demon possession is a process very similar to the process of accepting Christ, according to Southard. He believes that Christ and Satan both appear during times of vulnerability and great emotional lows in people's lives. The archetypal example that he uses is Satan's approach to Jesus in the wilderness tempting him with enticements from the world of power and physical pleasure. Here Satan waited until Jesus was at his weakest point in the forty-day fast and approached him with a grand scheme of surrendering his will to Satan in exchange for worldly power and pleasure. Southard believes that Satan approaches us, just as Satan approached Jesus, at our weakest moments. Jesus also comes, but Satan promises the "road most traveled," whereas Jesus promises the "road least traveled." Those who choose the road most traveled—surrendering their lives to Satan—become demon possessed and lose control over their lives. They become dominated and become oppressed.

I concur with Southard that demon possession is rare but real nevertheless. It involves a form of surrendering the self and the soul to external control and manipulation. It is a form of the sin of idolatry in which the negative forces of the world are activated.

Crossan's idea that demon possession is a protest or a revolt against domination makes sense. That is to say, people who demonstrate and manifest bizarre behavior may be symbolically indicating to the world that they are tired of the bondage and want out. It does seem plausible that such behavior, which is anti-social in nature, is a signal to authorities and to those outside the cult that there is something wrong and attention needs to be given to them and their activity.

It also seems plausible to me that there is a link between urban gang activity, occult practices, and antisocial activity. During the 1970s intervention by churches into gang activity seemed to help counter the hold that gangs had on youth and young adults.

Given the conclusion that demon possession is socially and theologically possible, it is appropriate to say something about shame, Jesus, and exorcism. First, shame feelings, such as unacceptableness and isolation, make people vulnerable to cult activity. Second, Jesus saw himself as helping people deal with their shame and shame-prone circumstances. Third, Jesus responded to those possessed the same way he responded to those who were sick or to those who were social outcasts. He engaged them with his personhood and his power of healing.

RETELLING THE STORY OF THE GERASENE DEMONIAC

The purpose of reviewing the cross-cultural anthropology of the Mediterranean world of Jesus, as well as the phenomenon of demon possession at other times and places, is to picture what demon possession would have been like for someone possessed during that time. The key is to get inside the mind and heart of the demon possessed person for the purposes of retelling the story. Retelling a story from pathos, or from the point of view of pity for the circumstances of the Gerasene demoniac, helps contemporary people with shame-based personalities to identify with the character of the Gerasene demoniac. In this identification it is hoped that the person will internalize the entire scene

89

in Mark 5, including Jesus' encounter with him. In doing this, the person will internalize a nurturing and transforming story that counteracts the original governing scene of shame that the person internalized.[10]

The key to the story of the Gerasene demoniac is the theme of domination and oppression. The story needs to proceed on the basis of presenting a setting that explicates the pitiful circumstance of the one possessed. The crucial fact to remember in telling the story is that the Gerasene demoniac sought out Jesus. Obviously, there was a real desire to change his own circumstances.

I grew up as a very angry man. I was not always demon possessed you know. I had a mother and a father. I got married and had a family. There was a hometown where people cared for one another. I miss that home environment. I really wish that I could go home but that is next to impossible now.

When I was a young man, anger got the best of me. I left home early because I did not want to be what my parents and community expected me to be. I had my own ambitions. I left home, striking out on my own, thinking that I eventually would find what I was looking for. Lonely and without anchoring in the community, I was very vulnerable. I wanted desperately to belong to a community, but it was not easy. I went to several synagogues, but they were like closed communities. There were, however, several groups that befriended me. I really didn't pay too much attention to them and what they did. All I knew was that they cared for me. They welcomed me into their fold and made me one of them.

They brought me into their community slowly. They used to have secret meetings late at night. Initially, they would not allow me to go into these meetings. At first I didn't mind. But then I began to wonder and ask questions about what they were doing. I wished that I would have never been so inquisitive. I found out far more than I wanted to. They told me that in order to get involved in that meeting I had to go through an initiation. I was excited that I might be moving closer into their inner circle. I will not say what the initiation involved. I am too ashamed to mention it. All I know is that I did things that were against the law. When I did them, this let them know that I was

COME OUT, YOU UNCLEAN SPIRIT

serious about being with them in their inner circle. I wish now that I would have never become involved with them.

The inner circle was nothing but ritual sacrifice using animals, as well as sexual acts that I had never before witnessed. The sacrifice and sexual acts were not normal, but I got heavily involved in them. Not long after getting involved in the inner circle, I was asked by the leader to do more and more things that I would have never thought of doing prior to leaving home. They were criminal acts. I could have been punished severely by the law if I were discovered, which I never was.

Before I knew it, I lost any respect that I had for myself. My life was not my own. I was at the leader's command. I was totally dominated, and I lost myself. I lost my agency. I was not a person anymore. I was controlled like a puppet on a string. I tried to leave several times, but they would find me and bring me back. I began to realize that there was no escape for me. I was doomed to a life of bondage, I thought.

Eventually, I became more and more antisocial. I began to stay away from the group. I began to stay in the graveyards. Increasingly, I became belligerent with the members in the group. I did not recognize who I was. All I knew was that I wanted to be left alone. I became so unruly that I was expelled from the group. People became afraid of me. Even the authorities could not handle me. I had the strength of a whole army of men. I had many things going on in my head that I could not control. The one hope that I had was that I could get back to my old self. I didn't like who I was at all.

Things began to change one day when I saw this group of people following this man. They were coming too close to where I was. I felt uncomfortable with them coming too close to where I lived. I thought that I would show myself and scare them off as I normally did when people got too close. Because of the state of mind that I was in, just looking at me would frighten people off. I heard someone in the crowd call the leader of the group Jesus. I thought I would direct my attention toward him. If I scared him, the rest would follow him and leave my turf.

I am looking back on things now since I am in my right mind. But back then I was not as calculating as I appeared to be. All I knew was that I had to get these people away from me, so that

I could feel all right. So I approached Jesus with my fiercest stuff. I looked the part of a crazy person. I screamed at the top of my voice. I ran at him like a mad man. I ran into tombstones trying to show them how powerful I was, but this man called Jesus was not frightened at all by my antics. He looked at me and my antics with pity. In fact, he told me to come closer to him. I was attracted by the invitation. Then, those demons inside of me took over. They recognized him immediately. They knew he was the Son of the Most High. They knew their time was up. They worried about what was going to happen to them. All I knew was that I began to envision that there might be a possibility of becoming whole again. So I was able to calm down and take control of my life, and I sat down and worshiped him. Those spirits in me did not like this. I saw my chance to be whole again in this man, and I was not going to let it slip away.

He began to speak to the spirits in me. He asked them what their names were. They responded "Legion," for there were so many of them. They begged him to leave them alone, but I wanted them out. He cast them out. They left me and went into a group of pigs. I was free for the first time in a long time. I was myself again for the first time in a long time. I listened to Jesus talk, and he made much sense to me. I decided that I wanted to become one of his followers, but he told me to go back home and tell them what he had done for me. I did what he told me to do, and I have been in my right mind ever since.

I found myself thinking, " 'I shall forever lift mine eyes to Calvary, to view the cross where Jesus died for me.' For if it were not for him, I would still be living among the tombs."[11] I thought further, "Prior to Jesus, hope had died in me. Now hope was springing eternally from the nurturing wells Jesus provided for me."

A CONTEMPORARY STORY OF DEMON INVOLVEMENT

I can say with confidence that I have never worked with a true case of demon possession in my ministry. I have, however, worked with people who felt that they had been victims of evil forces at work in their lives. They felt that there were no natural explanations that could adequately and fully account for what happened to them. Abnormal psychology was inadequate. Concepts like disassociated personality were totally inappropriate for them. Disassociation is a psychodynamic concept describing an ego-defense against anxiety internally generated in which the conscious mind attempts to exclude, deny, and separate itself from anxiety. Thus a part of the self is excluded in an attempt to control the anxiety. The part of the self that is excluded is called ego-alien in psychodynamic thinking because the split-off part of the self is considered to be foreign and alien. In my own mind there is no way to dismiss the idea of disassociation when a person has no history of contact with the occult. There is, however, a chance that demon possession is a possible explanation for someone's activities if a person was reared in a culture where demonology dominated the cultural worldview. Below is a story of such a possibility.

I was approached by an African woman who was a Christian but whose cultural background was dominated by a sophisticated worldview that included demons. She said that she was beatened and raped nightly by a demon, leaving her scared and tired every morning. She felt continually humiliated and abused by the demon.

I began to take down her history, believing that I was dealing with a very confused woman who was tormented by low self-esteem and mental illness. I discovered that she was well educated and had a very important job in her home country. She had received psychiatric help in her home country and was given medication here in the United States. Her family seemed not to have any outstanding mental problems. She was married, and I also had a meeting with her husband. He would not discuss the issue of demon possession, feeling that he had given up such ideas when he became Christian. I did find out, however, that he was not abusive toward her.

After finding out about her history of mental illness and medication, I referred her to a psychiatrist. He interviewed the woman, took her off her medication, and told me to help her to befriend the devil. I wondered what kind of medical recommendation this was. I felt helpless and did not know what he meant by befriending the devil. When I shared the psychiatrist's recommendations with the woman, she said that she did not want to befriend the devil. She said she wanted him gone. I felt I had no other choice than to help her befriend the devil. How to do this presented a real dilemma for me. There was no worldview available to me that gave me a clue to what it meant to become friendly with a demon. It was obvious to me that I had to do something since this woman was continually tormented, humiliated, and shamed every night and needed some immediate help.

I began to read up on exorcism. I decided that befriending meant casting out the demon. In order to understand the problem theologically and from a mainline Protestant tradition, I read John Richard's *Deliver Us from Evil.* Understanding the theology and practice related to exorcism from the Episcopalian standpoint would be more acceptable, given my background. Remember, my motivation was to try to relate to this woman's desperation.

After learning how to pray for the casting out of demons, I made up my mind that I was going to pray with this woman to cast out this demon. Later, I learned that I was not dealing with demon possession, but demon oppression. She was being harassed by the power of evil in her life. Exorcism, nevertheless, covers demon oppression as well. In my prayer I called on the power of the Holy Spirit to bind up the demon, to cast it out, to loose the woman from its power and influence, and I forbade it to return.

The woman began to report in subsequent counseling meetings that the devil had not disappeared, but it was neutralized. It had lost its power over her. It might show up at times, but it had no power to abuse or rape her. She was no longer terrorized by it. Correspondingly, her sense of humiliation and low self-esteem began to improve. She talked less of feeling worthless and flawed. She felt closer to God and to those with whom she worshiped.

CONCLUSION

While I was not convinced of the presence of the demon, I learned from this experience not to discount the power of demon oppression and demon possession in people's lives. The ritual of exorcism, under the right supervision, can be a real ally in pastoral counseling for those who have been involved in cults or in cultures where demonology is practiced.

Telling the above stories in preaching and pastoral counseling helps to create, in those who struggle with evil and demons in their lives, the hope of being healed from bondage and shame. Domination of any kind produces a sense of shame, and there are many resources for dealing with shame associated with evil and demons. My experience in preaching and counseling is that people feel relieved that the issue of demon possession and evil can be discussed. Many are reluctant to raise the issue about the subject because of fear of being misunderstood.

I did not abandon my ideas of disassociation. Nor did I decide exclusively for exorcism. Both dimensions are needed when dealing with mental and spiritual bondage and related shame.

PART THREE

SHAME AND
THE PARABLES
OF JESUS

In part 1, I paid close attention to how Jesus handled his own shame when others sought to humiliate him. I also explored the implications of his manner of handling shame for telling stories in pastoral counseling and preaching. In part 2, I explored Jesus' handling of the shame that others brought to him and how retelling these stories of Jesus can be an occasion for internalizing new scenes to replace the old, internalized, shame-based scenes. In part 3, I want to examine shame and the parables that Jesus told. The key focus will be on what Jesus believed God would be like in the new world he was inaugurating.

A major problem exists, however, when exploring the theme of shame in relation to parables. I have already established that Jesus' primary orientation was his conviction that the reign of God was rooted in a non-honor-and-shame-based paradigm with an egalitarian ethic. People's acceptance into God's rule and reign was not based on their class status or position or any external human standard rooted in in-group or out-group wisdom. Rather, inclusion was based on a new standard grounded in God's hospitality, acceptance, and generous grace to all who would accept them. The problem comes because Jesus used the metaphors of his shame and peasant background to show people the nature of God's new reign. Several questions arise at this juncture. The first is, Do not the metaphors Jesus borrowed from his Mediterranean common wisdom import the values from that culture? Second, if they do, might not the metaphors be contaminated, and therefore, would they be appropriate referents for understanding God's reign or kingdom?

There are two responses to these questions. First, to borrow metaphors from one arena of life and apply them to another is the stuff of theological method and discourse for Jesus, as well as for theologians throughout the ages. Jesus employed metaphors from the Mediterranean family, village, city, and beyond to make up his parables.[1] Jesus used familiar metaphors from the social world of his surroundings for his parables but obviously used them to the ends of understanding the nature of God's reign and God's new family.

The second response is that metaphors are literary vehicles or mediums that transcend time, space, and context and whose structures permit importing different content. In fact, Bernard Brandon Scott says that each parable plays out against the expectation of common wisdom, and a distinct and different voice emerges.[2] There is a contrast between the common wisdom of the day and the new way Jesus employed the metaphor in the parable. The contrast is between the distinctive voice that emerged when Jesus used the metaphor and the common wisdom of his surroundings. Jesus did not borrow the common wisdom. He employed the metaphor and employed radically new content.

It is my contention in part 3 that one criterion for identifying the authentic parables of Jesus is his continued critique of the shame-based common wisdom of his Mediterranean world and challenging people to embrace a new vision of reality that was unfolding. The thesis of part 3 is that the parables are short narrative stories about choosing to continue to live in the shame-based world or to orient one's life and self toward the approaching new reality of God's reign and family. A decision for the approaching new world meant growth and overcoming the problems associated with shame. Those who are oriented to the new and approaching world live by a different ethic as well. The mimetic implication is that our own retelling of parables in preaching and pastoral counseling needs to embrace the different voice of the approaching reign of God rather than the conventional shame-based wisdom of our day.

CHAPTER SEVEN

A PARENT WHO RISKS BEING SHAMED

"But while he was yet at a distance, his father saw him and had compassion, and ran and embraced him and kissed him."

(LUKE 15:20 RSV)

One of the dominant issues confronting life in the United States has to do with rediscovering parenting. There has been a reaction against the permissive parenting of the 1970s and 1980s, and this reaction focuses on the effort of men to take their rightful place in the home as fathers and husbands. President Clinton used the bully pulpit to highlight the problem of dead beat dads who deserted their children and refused to support them. The Promise Keepers movement, grounded in a patriarchal orientation, is trying to get males to reclaim their role as men in society. The Million Man March, initiated by the Black Muslim leader Louis Farrakhan, also seeks to help African American men to recover their lost role and rightful place in the home.

Those who watch trends in society and put them into some kind of perspective are saying that there is a paradigm shift occurring regarding fatherhood in our society. We are moving away from an incest narrative orientation grounded in the Freudian image of Oedipus Rex, who actually but unknowingly killed his father and married his mother. Replacing this antiparental myth in contemporary society is the Greek myth of Odysseus and Telemachus, in which Telemachus conspires with his recently returned father, the long-lost Odysseus, to thwart his mother's suitors.[1] This story helps to capture one of the dominant forces driving the lives of people today. This dynamic is the realization that commitment to the next generation will be one of the main rewards and contributions that one can make to society.

Generativity, or joyfully participating in the growth and develop-ment of the next generation, will be a dominant theme for the twenty-first century. We are, indeed, in a post-Freudian and post-antiparental age.

Though we are becoming more receptive to having a strong executive parental system in the home, the image of parenting that captures our imagination seems elusive. I want to suggest that Jesus' image of a parent who risks loss of honor in order to participate in the maturing process of a child is the appropriate image of parenting for today. For Jesus the father with two sons parable is about the parental nature of God, who launches adult children into the world and gives them the freedom to decide between the two worlds that exist, the present world or the world that is coming.

This chapter is about Jesus' faith in God as parent who risks loss of reputation and honor in order to participate in a loving way in the growth process of an adult child. The parable is not just about the life cycle transition between childhood and adult-hood. Rather, the parable is about the process of coming to faith, which is understood as a person orienting herself or himself to a nonshame-based world rather than grounding the self in an honor-and-shame-based world where value and worth are defined by position, prestige, power, and sex. In the shame-based world a person's worth is determined by meeting the expectation of oth-ers and following the customs of the family and community. In Jesus' new world, however, worth and value are gifts from God that come as a result of participating in God's coming new reign and rule.

HONOR IN FIRST-CENTURY FAMILIES

According to Bernard Brandon Scott's response to this parable (Luke 15:11-31), a first-century father put his family's name and honor in jeopardy by giving in to the younger son's request for his inheritance.[2] First, asking for one's inheritance was prema-ture, and to request the right of disposition of one's material legacy implied that the father was dead.[3] Second, the granting of the younger son's request threatened the family's honor or repu-tation because the father would be judged foolish for granting the son's request.[4] Third, the father looked even more foolish when the son lost all of his inheritance in riotous living, which jeopardized the family's material well-being.[5] Fourth, the younger son brought shame on the father's name because he participated in a forbidden profession that was not socially sanctioned by their religious faith. Working with pigs and eating food left for pigs made the younger son unclean and unfit for participation in the community.[6] In other words, he betrayed the family's honor and brought disgrace on the family by his unreasonable request and by his deplorable behavior in the world. His unfortunate behavior was reflected on his family's name.

Bruce Malina sheds additional light on the honor and shame system in Jesus' day. First, honor was defined by the value or worth one had in the eyes of others and one's social group.[7] Thus, worth and value in personhood were based on social acknowledgment. Such a view of value and worth make the dignity of the self socially determined. Worth in ancient Mediterranean culture was grounded in the power one had over others, in one's gender status, in roles of prestige and privilege, and in the influence one could amass. Respect and homage were paid to those who had all of these socially derived goodies.[8]

One's reputation was highly prized in first-century common wisdom.[9] Reputation was achieved by excelling and demonstrating one's superiority over others. Moreover, reputation was viewed as a scarce commodity, and one had to compete for superiority in order to win one's standing and reputation in the community.[10] Reputation and honor were only reserved for a small group of people; therefore, competition was fierce. There were few winners but many losers. Many were disgraced, few were honored. To gain and then to lose honor was a significant tragedy.

Protecting one's honor and reputation against affront from outside the family was paramount in this ancient culture. Punishment for affronting a person of honor was severe.[11] The challenge of one's honor by an inferior was not tolerated. Only equals could challenge one's honor.

Family honor was also very important. Protecting the family name from dishonor was highly prized. Marriage was viewed as the fusion of the honor and reputation of two extended families.[12] Thus, anything that would bring dishonor to the two families was to be avoided at all costs.

With respect to the parable of the father with two sons, the family's reputation and name were at stake because of the younger son's insistence on the division of the family's wealth. Parenting was viewed as controlling one's own and preventing family members from engaging in ruinous activities. A parent permitting a child to challenge the family's social image was deemed stupid and foolish. For a parent to indulge a son's unreasonable request as it was presented in the parable was socially and economically flirting with disaster.

The point is that Jesus was constantly challenging the conventional shame-and-honor-based culture of his day in a variety of ways. Through parables he was introducing a new system of evaluating human worth and dignity. His orientation was not anchored in what was obvious but was rooted in what was coming to people from the future of God's reign and rule. This new future was an egalitarian community in which the worth of persons was bestowed as a gift from God rather than as something generated by society. Thus, for Jesus, personal worth transcended social custom. Human worth and value did not depend on the vulnerability of one's reputation or the fragility of one's accrued honor.

With this new, transcendent understanding of worth and honor, Jesus could tell a story of a father who was able to risk his honor and reputation for the sake of an adult child's destiny and well-being. The father was viewed as having another source of assessing reality than the one provided by wider society. His different orientation provided him with the necessary courage to appropriate and actualize a completely novel way of relating to adult children.

A VIEW FROM THE PSYCHOLOGY OF SHAME

As already indicated, the internalization of the social valuation of the self is something that is not peculiar to the first century. How one is perceived in the eyes of others is still a major force and dynamic in contemporary life as well. Although individualism and theories of self view maturity as a process of extricating one's center of evaluation from social expectation and putting it within the person, the maturation process begins with the expectations of others. To become a mature self in the parlance of modern psychology and family systems theory is a long process of personal unfolding and interpersonal interaction in which the individual moves between inner goals and socially sanctioned goals. Eventually, a mature person becomes self-differentiated and can distinguish the self from others and can own his or her uniqueness as well as similarity with others.

Contemporary emphasis on the social construction of reality and on the social context of behavior helps us to realize that social and cultural values and expectations are always at work in human growth and development. We deceive ourselves if we think otherwise. Consequently, it is impossible to avoid expectations that are rooted in forms of shame and honor.

Parenting expectations seem to be one of those areas where shame and honor expectations and values dominate. It does appear that the same honor and shame principles of valuation are at work, particularly with regard to our understanding of dysfunctional parenting, parental abuse, and addictive relationships. The point is that caregiving professionals must report cases of child abuse in most states, and this state of affairs has forcefully brought to our awareness the need to have high public expectations for parenting. The fascination of the media with the private lives of the rich and famous and the vulnerability in their relationships is also an indication that honor and shame valuation is not dead.

Perfectionism and the demand for it in parenting today seems to be on the rise.[13] Perfectionism with regard to parenting, the expectation that one can achieve completeness as a parent, is emerging as one of the major shame-based evaluating systems today. For example, Jesse Jackson, at the 1997 American Association of Marriage and Family Counselors meeting in Atlanta, said: "I have five children, and I don't love any of them equally. I love them adequately. Some need more love than others." The point is that there is a social expectation that good parenting is loving children equally and not showing partiality. In short, human worth as a parent is being increasingly defined as how well we carry out our parenting tasks. Our worth as human beings is being defined by the quality of parenting we offer our children.

While expectations of parents are very important in helping us to set norms for our behavior as parents, determining our worth and value as human beings based on our behavior as parents is very risky. The danger is that we might make global self-attributions, in Michael Lewis's sense, if we fail to meet our own expectation.[14] That is, people who are not adequate parents will tend to view themselves as worthless because they do not meet the norms of perfect or good parenting. Success as parents is very tenuous today, and the expectation of being the ideal parent is too intimidating. Jesse Jackson is correct. We need to be adequate parents, and we need to find our source of self-evaluation in something that transcends social expectations of us as parents.

A THEOLOGICAL VIEW AND MIMETIC IMPLICATIONS

We are to follow the norms of parenting laid out by our faith tradition. We are to be caring and selfless parents for the sake of the unfolding reign of God. This is our ethical and moral responsibility and expectation. This is to be our response to God's gift of personhood and grace. Our worth as persons is not determined by our meeting these norms of living. Rather, our worth is given to us as a gift, and our loving of others is our response to what has been given as a gift. We are not to keep the gift of worth as a private possession, but we are to share it with others so that they too can know the love of God. To ground our self-evaluation in our success or failure in carrying out our ethical and moral responsibility as parents is to practice idolatry. That is, our self-worth is not a result of works but of grace. Whether good parents, adequate parents, or poor parents, we still are people of worth in God's eyes.

RETELLING THE STORY OF THE FATHER WITH TWO SONS

In an honor-and-shame-based culture, most people will identify with the elder son's attitude. Most of us, particularly if we play life by the rules and social expectations, would have strong feelings about the graceful way the father treated the younger son in the parable. We often resent the fact that the younger son got rewarded for breaking the rules. The parable, however, is about more than rewarding the breaking of rules. The parable is calling into question our principles of self-valuation. Therefore, our attention should be on the elder son and his honor and shame orientation. He was loyal to the honor and shame system of his day. Those who identify with the elder son might also be more vulnerable to shame. That is, the self-valuation mechanism of those who identify with the elder son might make them more prone to shame if they fail.

Given the vulnerability of those of us who identify with the elder son, it will be important to retell this ancient story of a father with two sons from the point of view of the elder son. The main reason for doing this is to focus on how those of us who ground our self-worth in the expectations of others can find an alternative way of self-evaluation.

I don't understand why my father would risk all he had for this brother of mine. It is unheard of for a son to ask for his inheritance prior to the death of the father. To ask such a thing is the same as pronouncing my father dead. To ask what my younger brother asked for jeopardizes the entire family's economic well-being. If that were not enough, it also threatens to ruin the reputation and honor of my father's good name. When people find out what he did and how he indulged his younger son, his good name will be turned into derision and ridicule. He will be the brunt of many jokes and laughs. Why would my father risk so much? The stakes were tremendously high. What my father did was unprecedented.

To make matters even worse, my brother went and squandered every penny that was given to him. The fact that my father divided up the inheritance almost bankrupted the family, but when the money was lost by my brother, this also meant that the entire family lost as well. The youngster is so self-centered and stupid. Why didn't my father anticipate these revolting developments and stop this disaster before it started? The family name is ruined. Do you see what havoc this boy has visited on us?

When you think that things could not get worse and that

things are beginning to take a favorable new turn, the bottom falls out again. Word came to us that the youngster had hired himself out to an unsanctioned profession, one that has been forbidden by our religious faith. He worked with the unclean pigs and ate what they eat. How horrible! The family cannot show itself in the synagogue now without the turning of heads and negative gossip. I am so deeply upset at my father for what he did.

My father's crowning humiliating act was to make a big deal of my brother's return home. He threw this big party as if my brother had gone off and become some great hero. If you want my father's love, it looks like you have to go out and destroy the family name. Then you will be rewarded. What kind of logic is this?

I asked my father what on earth could have persuaded him to do what he was doing? His response to me was very disturbing. He said that there was nothing on earth that could have caused him to do what he did. Respectfully, I said, "I cannot understand your logic." He responded that my brother had lost his way and was almost destroyed by the world, but he finally awakened and found his way. He was immature, now he is mature. He knows where to anchor and ground his life now, my father said. He continued that it was worth losing his wealth in order for his youngest son to find his way in life. He said that no price is too high to pay for the well-being of any of his children. He also made me feel better when he said he would do the same thing for me.

I think I am getting it now. What my dad was saying was that he would risk everything in order to save his children. This is a new and revolutionary way of thinking. It is definitely not the conventional way of thinking.

As we noted earlier, Jesus' parables challenge the conventional wisdom and expectations of the honor and shame system. Parables often introduce expectations that reverse the normal expectations of society. The role of the parable is to challenge the wisdom of society and introduce an alternative view of life.

TELLING A CONTEMPORARY STORY

The following story was told by a student after I read the above story of the father with two sons.

Between adolescence and young adulthood my parents had very little control over me. They were very strict when I was growing up. I could not wait to get out from under their watchful eyes.

When I went to college, this was my opportunity to experiment and do the things I wanted to do. I tried not to associate with the kinds of friends my parents approved of when I was in high school. In high school my friends were studious, safe, and very serious about life. I hung out with them because I knew this would please my parents. Somehow, I always wanted to please them and never upset them. When I went to college and experienced being on my own for the first time, I decided that I was going to really see what I had been missing when I was living at home. My friends in college were fast; they were into the party scene more than studying; they drank and smoked pot, or marijuana.

Rather than studying, I spent most of my time living the fast life and wasting my parent's hard-earned money. I literally went wild. I tried everything: sex, drugs, alcohol.

I really was not ready for the drug and alcohol scene. I always felt shy and passive. Drugs and alcohol made me more sociable and less shy. I needed those substances to feel secure when I was around others. I always wanted to be popular and outgoing, and the drugs and alcohol allowed me to be more outgoing. Soon, I found that I could not do without the drugs and alcohol. I was slowly becoming a junkie.

When I would come home from college, I felt as if I needed to be the new self I had developed and show my parents that I did not have to live by their rules and expectations. I could tell they were disappointed, but they allowed me to keep whatever schedule I wanted to. Sometimes I would stay out all night. Even though they said nothing, I knew they were concerned.

I had some serious problems kicking substance abuse. After some counseling and dealing with a twelve-step program, I was able to live without drugs or drinking. I think the turning point came for me when I accidentally found out that when I was out late at night, my mother would bring her pillow downstairs and sleep by the front door until she heard my footsteps. Then she would get up and go to bed.

In my mind, this meant that my mother cared that I become

an adult, no matter how much of a mess I made of my life. It meant that she was with me and had the patience to be there for me even when she disapproved of my behavior. She only told me what she did when she knew I had finally found my way and straightened out my life. She wanted to come and take over my life, but she resisted, knowing that I had to find my way without her intervention. I am glad she was by the door praying for me. I am also glad she allowed me to find my own way.

Good parenting is letting go when it is time for the young adult to leave home and become an adult, no matter how hard it is. When I was a child, I used to hear sermons about how the eagle stirred the nest so that the eaglets could learn to fly when it was time. She would not let them fall, but she would systematically dismantle the nest so that the eaglets would know that they could not stay forever in the nest. The mother eagle stirred the nest and watched patiently for her children to fly. The point was that God was like the mother eagle who wanted us to grow and mature when it was time, even though it may have been difficult. Not letting us go and experience life and our own choices would not be effective parenting for launching young adults. In the parable of the father with two sons, God is symbolized by an effective parent who acted outside the ordinary expectation of parents so that the young adult could find himself.

WHEN TO TELL STORIES IN PASTORAL COUNSELING

I have discovered that many people have to work through many difficult feelings about their parents. Some are so angry at their parents that they cannot identify or recover any nurturing scenes or events with regard to their parents. However, there are times when glimpses of nurture may occur to them unexpectedly. This would be a good time to reinforce these remembered nurturing moments with a story, particularly in pastoral counseling.

There are also times when people find it hard to see how certain behaviors of their parents were loving, much in the same way that the elder son had difficulty envisioning the care of his father in the parable. Sometimes these stories can be told in pastoral counseling to help people see the care of their parents when they resist seeing something positive that actually exists.

CHAPTER EIGHT

HOSPITALITY
AT A COST

"Go therefore to the thoroughfares, and invite to the marriage feast as many as you find."

(MATTHEW 22:9 RSV)

First Sunday in the denominational tradition in which I grew up was extremely important. With nearly the stature of Easter and Mother's Day, first Sunday marked the largest attendance at church every month. First Sunday was paramount because it symbolized God's "Welcome Table." The "Welcome Table" in the African American Christian tradition was symbolic of the hospitality of God, whose openness extended the banquet invitation to "whosoever will." All, regardless of color or gender, were invited to God's eternal banquet. Because God sent out a general invitation to all humanity, no human being had the power to revoke the hospitality of God.

In the Jesus debate, table associations marked the point where Jesus chose to challenge the social customs regarding honor and shame. The occasions of eating were times when Jesus introduced the eschatological expectation about what life would be like in God's rule and reign. African Americans, especially, know about this open banquet, and God's hospitality has become an important dimension in their struggle for freedom and liberation in a shame-and-honor-based culture.

This chapter will explore the parable of the Banquet Invitation in light of first-century Mediterranean honor and shame wisdom. We will also pay close attention to the distinction between global attributions and specific attributions with regard to shame.

INSIGHTS FROM SCHOLARSHIP

In Matthew 22:2-14 and Luke 14:16-24 the host gives up any privileged status and assumes the status of ordinary people. The parable is about the host refusing to adopt the class standards of that day and making sure that the peasant class or "whosoever will" is invited to the banquet.

It is thought that Luke's account of the banquet is closer to the authentic parable because it preserves the appropriate social context of Jesus' day.[1] Bernard Brandon Scott points out that Matthew's theological and ideological concerns are prevalent; thus, Matthew's additions to the parable alter its meaning.[2] Luke's account, however, seems to preserve the themes of concern for the poor and conflict with the religious leaders that characterize most of the parables.[3] The concern for honor is also a major dimension of the parable, so that the humble are exalted to a place of honor. Here again we are reminded that Jesus often used table associations to talk about what life will be like in the reign of God. At the banquet table, there will be the poor, the maimed, and the blind.

Of crucial importance in Luke's presentation of the parable is the host's loss of status, because the original invited guests snubbed the banquet and its host. Scott points out that the parable depicts the host losing upper-class status and power by associating with those of lesser status from the streets.[4] There is no way for the host to raise the status of the poor. The host has to join the poor, Scott concludes. In short, the parable shows that salvation is not about elevation in class status but entrance into the reign of God. Scott says:

> The Jesus parable, like the parable A Grain of Mustard Seed, works by misdirection. One expects a messianic banquet to parallel the cedar of Lebanon, but one ends up with a householder's feast filled with the uninvited, with those who will give him no honor. The parable reverses and subverts the system of honor. The man who gives a banquet loses his honor and joins the shameless poor. An audience expects the messianic banquet to signal that those who have suffered at the hands of Israel's enemies will be restored to honor by the power of God. Here the opposite happens.[5]

In the parable of the father with two sons (Luke 15:11-32) the story points to God risking the actual loss of honor. In this parable about a banquet of the poor, God takes a step beyond risk and is actually portrayed as losing honor by radically identifying with the poor. This parable suggests the theological doctrine of the incarnation in which a part of the Triune God divests the Self of all divine privilege in order to save humankind.

The apostle Paul also picks up a version of this theme of God choosing what was weak to shame the strong and what was foolish to shame the wise (1 Cor. 1:18-25). The point is that our salvation and our identity do not come from our allegiance to the world's standards of honor, in Paul's mind or in the mind of the writer of Luke. Salvation is a gift from God as we are invited to the eternal feast and accept the invitation.

INSIGHTS FROM THE PSYCHOLOGY OF SHAME

Most of the parables make a statement about global attributions in the sense that they deal with those who have internalized the values of the social class to which they belonged in first-century Mediterranean culture. Luke's concern is to make sure that those who believe themselves unwelcome at the feast because of status are actually invited. In first-century Mediterranean culture those who were from the upper class and lower classes would not expect the host to do what the host did. Yet, the parable is very clear that the social convention was reversed.

Those who accepted the invitation did not receive elevated social standing. Rather, they received the gift of acceptance. Their global attributions based on internalizing the social standards of the day were challenged. They still may not be privileged in the social realm, but in the spiritual realm they are valuable and worthwhile.

MIMETIC IMPLICATIONS

There are two issues that the parable of the banquet addresses. The first is that of those whose shame makes them feel left out of God's life and plan. The second deals with those who expect God to restore the social honor that was lost.

It is clear that those people who feel that they are left out and forgotten can now believe and hope that they are no longer excluded but are very much a part of God's plan and family. This is true whether society changes its way of valuing or not. Spiritual acceptance means a lot, and those who have it are to live their lives differently based on the knowledge that they are worthwhile. Acceptance of the invitation to the banquet means that one takes on the value that God gives as a gift and that one lives life according to the egalitarian standards of the reign of God. Thus, self-treatment and other-treatment take seriously the family ethics of God's family, in which all persons are viewed as valuable and are treated with respect and equality. "Let this mind be in you, which was also in Christ Jesus" here refers to feeling positive about oneself and treating others the same way Jesus treated people.

With regard to those who expect to be restored to the honor and status that the world bestows as a result of being invited to the banquet, the mimetic implication is clear. The parable is not about restoring honor or class status. It is about restoring human dignity and worth. People who enter the banquet are expected to give up their allegiance to the values of conventional wisdom and accept the values of the egalitarian ethic. To put the message in modern terms, God does not save people from shame and guilt so that they can be middle class. Rather, God saves people to participate in the unfolding egalitarian world where God is ruling and reigning.

Some people with shame-based problems expect that those who did the shaming ought to be punished. John Patton, in his book *Is Human Forgiveness Possible?* talks about those who become self-righteous and begin to pursue with vengeance anyone who has shamed them or has the potential of shaming them.[6] The point he is making is that some people who have shame protect themselves from being overwhelmed by it by becoming shame police, trying to pursue those who shame others and punish them. Accepting the invitation to the banquet means that one leaves such worldly concerns alone and lives by new standards.

WHO IS GOD IN THE PARABLES?

As indicated earlier, Scott believes that Matthew's theological agenda overrides the authentic meaning of the parable. For him

Matthew's concern is with people's rejection of God's reign and what will result because of this rejection.[7] The theme of judgment is very much a part of Matthew's concern for those who do not accept the reign of God.

Because of this judgment theme, Scott feels that the most authentic parable is Luke's account. Luke, Scott feels, preserves the most realistic and authentic parable. It is my contention that there are two different pictures of God presented here, as well. Matthew's theology pictures a vengeful and angry God while Luke presents a God who is in solidarity with those who are poor and suffer from shame. In Matthew, God is concerned about God's own honor and protecting status, whereas Luke portrays God giving up status in order to care for and transform those who suffer from shame.

This contrast is very important for those whose images of God are primarily those of judgment and revenge. There are those who come to church believing that they will be punished for their sins and that punishment is high on God's list. Rather than having realistic shame about their specific behavior, they have a more toxic shame in the sense that they have made global attributions about their worthlessness. Global shame overrides specific shame related to behavior. These people need to know more about Luke's banquet. Those who have a positive sense of self and have done specific sins might need to hear Matthew's account of the banquet.

Below I recommend telling both parables and leaving the decision of which God appeals the most to the hearer. I have in mind one person whose global shame was dominant but who felt that God's wrath was coming down hard on her. Telling the story of the two parables could perhaps help open up the several images of God that these parables address.

RETELLING MATTHEW 22:1-14

In this section I will first tell Matthew's version of the banquet, and then I will tell Luke's version. The goal is to make sure that those who hear the parables have a contrast. Often in counseling there are those whose shame prevents them from visualizing themselves being invited to the banquet. It is much easier for them to see themselves being put out of the banquet if invited. Thus, telling both stories, one after the other, provides a basis for the counselee or parishioner to ponder the nature of God in relationship to his or her feelings of shame.

Of course, there is no way of knowing what the parishioner or counselee will do with the two stories once they are told. However, narrative storytelling trusts the process of the story engaging the person and the person engaging the story. One major difference between pastoral counseling and preaching is that it is possible to get feedback almost immediately from how the counselee is utilizing the story. In preaching this is not always possible. It is hoped that there could be a forum where people could explore their concerns following preaching.

> A host gave a banquet for his son. He sent his servants to invite people to the feast. Those who were invited refused to come. The host sent out the servants a second time, and those invited refused to come a second time. This time, however, some ridiculed the hosts and the servants; others had other business; and another group seized and killed the servants. The host was very angry, and he pursued and destroyed the murderers with his army. The host declared that those who had been invited were not worthy, so he sent the servants out a third time to invite anyone who would come, whether worthy or unworthy, to the marriage feast.
>
> The wedding party was full, and the host came to view the guests who came to the banquet feast. He noticed that there was someone there without the appropriate wedding garment, and this person was thrown out of the marriage feast.

RETELLING LUKE 14:16-24

I will retell this story from the point of view of the servant who was sent out by the host to recruit people for the banquet.

> My employer sent me to invite people to the banquet. He made special arrangements, and we worked several days simply to make sure everything was just right. My employer was definite about who to invite to the banquet. There were those who were part of the regular banquet goers. They got invitations to

all the important banquets around town. They were the very important people, or VIPs. You had to have these people at the banquet, and they would be at the head table. They would receive special invitations. These people would be upset if they were not given special attention and special recognition at the banquet. Some of them liked to make grand entrances into the banquet room by having their name announced.

When I went to the homes of the VIPs, to my surprise every one of them had an excuse for not coming. I will not elaborate on these excuses except to say that they all seemed to have conspired together to make up similar excuses. It seemed to me that they did not want to come to the banquet, as if it were beneath their class status to come. At least it seemed to me that it was not worth their effort to try to attend. The reasons that they gave for not wanting to come did not sound authentic to me.

When I told my employer about the refusal of the VIPs to come, he said that the banquet must go on; the preparations must not go to waste. He said to go back out into the streets and invite anyone who would come. Include the crippled, the poor, the outcasts, and the not-so-VIP. His words were "whosoever will, let them come."

At first I responded 'to my employer in the form of a question, for I had some concerns about what he was doing. I guess I was trapped by the values of the community. My question was, "Do you know that this means you have been snubbed by the VIPs, and your inviting any and everybody to your banquet will not gain you any favor with those of the upper crust of society?" My employer indicated that he was very aware of what his decision meant and its consequences. He said he was willing to live with the consequences since his life was more than trying to win the favor of some group. His concern, he said, was to make sure that all people had an opportunity to participate in the banquet feast, and the invitation had to go out to all, regardless of their social or economic status. With this open invitation in my mind, I gladly went out to execute my employer's wishes.

A CONTEMPORARY RETELLING

The following story is one that I developed from working with a counselee over a full year during which we had many conversations about God. She had a basic conviction that God hated her because of the sins she committed in her life. Her shame was based on global attributions of unlovability. Her feelings of being unloved by God were activated by the loss of her father, whom she said was the only person who loved her. She felt that God had taken him from her as punishment for her sins. She felt that if she continued to sin, God would also take her children from her. This story can be told to people who bring with them a basic belief that God is punitive and rewards sin with wrath rather than love and forgiveness. This person was aware of the two banquet stories and their differences.

I remember the two stories you told me in counseling. I have been thinking about them all week. I am glad you told me both of them. I can't believe that God would invite me to a banquet without some strings attached. The things I have done are so bad and shameful, there is no way God would ever send out an invitation to me. If God were to break down and invite me, I would be the one who would be excluded because I would not have on the right banquet clothes.

There is no way God would allow me at that banquet. Under no circumstances would God let me in. I have done some real evil things in my day. Even if I repent, there can be no hope for me in God's mind. Why should I give up what I believe about God's judgment of me? I would rather hold on to my attitude about God. This way I can go on living the life I prefer. I know I am unforgivable; therefore, I don't have to change. It would do no good. I don't want to do anything differently; it is more convenient now for me to believe God hates me. To be unloved is easier for me to swallow than being loved. It is more predictable. The case is closed.

You ask about my father. Why do you bring him up? I was the apple of his eye. I am sorry he died. When he died, something died in me as well. My world changed forever. I haven't been the same since. If God loved me so much, why did he take away the one who loved me? God was cruel to me. He punishes you by taking away people you love and who love you. I am so angry at God for how he has treated me. I really don't want to go to the banquet. God has another trick up his sleeve. He just wants to get at me again and hurt me. I don't really trust God. I know I will be punished for saying this. I can't win.

Do I trust anyone, is that your question? Since my father died I trust no one. Sometimes, however, my father's presence comes over me, especially when I am in trouble or when I am about to do something stupid. I guess my father's spirit is still alive. I feel real good when he visits me. These are the only times that I feel loved.

If I allow myself to go to the banquet, you say, I could feel this feeling of love more often. This is an interesting possibility. I am not quite ready to accept your conclusion. I am not ready to admit that it is God who is loving me through the appearance of my father. I will ponder this more. It is too much to consider now. If this is true, this could turn my life around. I am not quite ready to do that just yet. I don't want to be disappointed by God again. It is emotionally safe not to expect very much from God. God stole my father from me, and I am not ready to let God off the hook just yet.

CONCLUSION

Jesus used parables to introduce unexpected and novel ideas. For a person to be loved in spite of his or her sins was a revolutionary idea for the first-century Mediterranean world. Obvious in the second banquet story is the belief that God only judges and punishes sinners. From the woman in the contemporary retelling of the story, we can see that this belief in a punishing God is not confined to antiquity. Such a belief is alive and thriving even today.

Many of the parables, with some exceptions, are stories that challenge the honor and shame culture of Jesus' day. They can also be used in similar ways today. Knowing that we are loved despite our being unacceptable is very critical to most of us, and the parable can be used to convey this message today. When the parable is used in pastoral counseling and in preaching, the negative convictions about ourselves can be challenged and new ideas can be introduced.

CONCLUSION

T his chapter will make some final comments about the appropriate use of stories in pastoral counseling and preaching. The goal here is to reinforce some of the ideas that have been presented already. Also, I want to make a statement about how telling and retelling stories enables us to learn by appropriating the patterns and ideas provided us by our faith tradition.

NARRATIVE CHALLENGES NEGATIVE
BELIEFS AND CONVICTIONS

The first idea that I want to highlight is that narrative has the ability to address the strongly held beliefs and convictions that shape our lives in negative ways. Much of what Crossan says about the function of parables can be said for the function of narratives in preaching and pastoral counseling. For Crossan, parables challenge the expectations that people bring with them to a situation by means of presenting alternative expectations. With regard to shame, this means that the convictions about one's being unacceptable and worthless are challenged by opposite beliefs. Thus, when stories are written, they need to be written in such a way that they introduce the common or usual expectation; then the story needs to challenge that expectation; and finally, the story needs to introduce a healing, alternative expectation.

Permit me to use an illustration that comes vividly to my mind.

I once conducted the funeral of a young woman. She was in her early thirties. She committed suicide, and according to all those who knew her well, she did it because she finally gave up fighting an eating disorder. She was a perfectionist, and this perfecionism focused on her eating. She was a very thin person, but in her own eyes she was not acceptable. She suffered toxic shame, believing that she was completely flawed and worthless because she could not be satisfied with herself and her body image.

My concern in the funeral sermon was to address the concerns of those who survived the tragedy. There were concerns that I knew the grieving loved ones were raising. They all felt that there was something that they could have done to prevent the suicide. They all believed they were responsible in some way. Many also had religious concerns about what would happen to the soul of the loved person who committed suicide. Thus, I wanted to provide a meaningful service and sermon that could address both the guilty feelings they had as well as their concerns about the soul of their loved one.

It was also important to me to help people see the suicide as faulty thinking about shame issues. In this particular case, the shame had to do with failure to meet society's expectations regarding the ideal feminine body image. I wanted to make sure that those who attended the funeral were aware of the social and cultural factors that helped to activate the suicide. I realized that there were some interpersonal factors that motivated the suicide, as well. One of these contributing factors was internalized expectations from childhood, and I wanted to lay the ground work for challenging these internalized expectations as well.

I chose to use the story of the sinful woman who bathed the feet of Jesus with her tears and hair in Luke 7, believing that this story captured the challenge that I wanted to provide for the grieving love ones. I emphasized that the woman's sins were not identified. Also the presence of Simon represented the voice of honor and shame in society. The key points that I wanted the story to address were several. First, I wanted to introduce the idea that the grievers did not have to worry about the soul of the departed because the same story was currently being enacted between the deceased and God. I wanted to emphasize that the soul of the departed was being cared for by God. Second, I wanted the story to show how personal worth is a gift from God rather than a reward for being successful or perfect. Third, the deceased woman had a very kind heart, and the story was an appropriate metaphor for the way she actually showed hospitality to others and the way her life was worthwhile, even though she did not believe it was. I felt that the story of the woman who was forgiven because of her love and hospitality was appropriate to accomplish the goals that I thought needed to be achieved for those who brought their guilt and shame to the funeral.

The funeral context also gave me an opportunity to communicate the points that I wanted to make after telling the story. The counseling context, however, may not present the same opportunity in quite the same way. The same story could be told in pastoral counseling, but the implications of the story for those suffering loss might be explored in a different way. In preaching the preacher can use the story, knowing what most people are feeling based on his or her experience and knowledge of the grief reaction. In pastoral counseling, however, the pastoral counselor must wait for the appropriate time to tell the story based on the readiness of the counselee. It is not clear when the counselee will begin to raise the kinds of questions that can be raised in the context of the funeral. The pastoral counselor needs to understand the grieving process and not introduce the story prematurely. Prematurely introducing the story may interrupt the process of healing that occurs. Using stories in the funeral, however, can help to frame the questions people have so that when the time for raising them in a one-to-one counseling relationship arises, there may be some bases for the conversation.

Death vividly calls to our awareness the shame issue that confronts us today. Death also helps us to see how important telling stories is both in preaching and in pastoral care and counseling. Death is a vivid illustration for focusing the prevalence of shame in our culture today. There are, however, many activators of shame, including losses and failures of many kinds. In addressing the shame from these losses and failures, both preaching and pastoral counseling are essentially related, working hand in glove. While they occur in different settings, there is significant overlap between them that cannot be ignored. They are both essential to effectively challenge the shame that we experience. They serve as vehicles for conveying God's grace and love, which is the source of our feelings of worth and value.

IMITATION AND REPETITION AS THE BASIS
FOR DEALING WITH SHAME

Let this mind be in you (Phil. 2:5) is a convenient biblical phrase for expressing the possibility of emulating the attitude Jesus had toward himself despite shaming experiences in his life. It is based on the belief that what Jesus felt is repeatable. The idea of repetition or repeating past possibilities as vehicles to present novelty and creation forms the theological and philosophical bases of how we grow and change as human beings.

Theologically, the tradition of mimicking or imitating the behavior of Jesus is well established. The early church, especially Paul, believed that imitating Jesus' behavior and his attitude were central to what it meant to be Christian. Thus, how Jesus handled his own personal shame and the shame that others had was something that can be imitated by his followers.

Idealist philosophy thought that ideas and patterns are universally repeatable in the lives of people. Thus, Plato, Kierkegaard, Kant, and Jung, all personalistic and process thinkers, recognized that patterns and forms for bringing life meaning exist and are repeatable. Novelty and creativity depend on these repeatable patterns even though the content of the patterns changes. These patterns are archetypes that make living, meaning, and possibility real.

Parables often serve as a form or repeatable pattern for introducing novelty and possibility when shame dominates our lives. Storytelling is also a repetitious pattern that serves the end of introducing new possibility despite shame. The pastoral counseling relationship and preaching are settings where the repetition is enacted. Through story and parable, people with shame can reenact scenarios of possibility that lead to creative living.

Shame is not the final word. Vehicles exist for transforming shame into positive meaning. Preaching and pastoral counseling are important and essential vehicles in this transforming process.

NOTES

INTRODUCTION

1. To determine the authentic teachings of Jesus has long been a problem for biblical scholarship. Separating the authentic sayings of Jesus from what the writers of each of the Gospels said about Jesus is no easy task. Therefore, knowing what Jesus felt about himself, his ministry, and his relationships with others presents a real problem.

This work relies primarily on the intellectual efforts of several scholars, the first of which is Joachim Jeremias' book, *New Testament Theology* (New York: Charles Scribner's Sons, 1971). In it he points to the problems we encounter when trying to recapture the authentic words of Jesus. For example, there is no record of even a single line of scripture that came from Jesus' own hand. Noting that more than thirty years elapsed before anything Jesus said was actually recorded, Jeremias indicates that alterations to what Jesus actually said must have occurred. Jeremias works out an elaborate method for rediscovering the authentic words of Jesus, and his results are plausible for our purposes. Basically, his method involves the *criterion of dissimilarity,* through which he seeks to find the earliest tradition in which a saying of Jesus cannot be traced to Judaism or the early church.

What I like about Jeremias's conclusions is that it is possible to discern what Jesus believed about himself, his relationships with others, and his ministry. Jesus' sayings are significant theological statements that encompass a wide variety of topics organized significantly around the dawning of the kingdom of God or rule of God. Therefore, I will rely on some of Jeremias's observations about Jesus' authentic sayings as I seek to attend to the beliefs and convictions of Jesus.

I also find the work of John Dominic Crossan very helpful in my attempt to find the authentic sayings of Jesus. His book, *Jesus: A Revolutionary Biography* (San Francisco: Harper, 1994), tries to reconstruct the authentic beliefs and convictions of Jesus by exploring cross-cultural anthropology. He examines ancient Mediterranean agrarian culture, which he views as distinct from contemporary industrial society; first-century Greco-Roman and Jewish history; and the total collection of material compiled about Jesus inside and outside the canon. The conclusions he makes relevant to the concern of this book are:

(1) Jesus was a Jewish peasant, and (2) his strategy for himself and his followers involved a combination of healing, common eating, and a form of religious and economic egalitarianism that negated the hierarchical and patronal culture that was common to Jewish religion and Roman power. His egalitarianism was grounded in unmediated spiritual contact with God and others, which he announced was a sign of the presence of the kingdom of God. Everything that Jesus did and said—his miracles, his sayings, his parables, his healing, and his eating—served the end of undermining a shame and honor based society in which some were considered more valuable than others. I will explore Crossan's conclusions about the peasant culture in which Jesus carried out his ministry and how Jesus' ministry was oriented to deal with that shame-based culture. By *shamed-based* I am referring to a culture in which people's value and worth are determined by their status and position in society. Part of what Crossan helps me to say is that Jesus saw himself as a person of worth, despite his social standing and position.

Helping us focus on what we need to emulate from Jesus is the work of Marcus J. Borg, *Jesus A New Vision: Spirit, Culture, and the Life of Discipleship* (San Francisco: Harper and Row, 1987). This work focuses on Jesus' relationship with the Spirit as a central dimension of his work and on Jesus' relationship to culture. From Borg's picture of the historical Jesus, we can glimpse more of what our own relationship to the Spirit and to the world around us can be. Other biblical scholars from whose work I draw include John P. Meier and Bernard Brandon Scott.

2. Michael E. Williams, *Storytellers Companion to the Bible*, vol. 2 (Nashville: Abingdon, 1992), 11.

3. Renita Weems, *Just a Sister Away: A Womanist Vision of Women's Relationships in the Bible* (San Diego: LuraMedia, 1988).

4. The construction of reality is referred to in the work of Peter Berger and Robert Luckmann, *The Social Construction of Reality: A Treatise in the Sociology of Knowledge* (Garden City, N.Y.: Doubleday, 1966).

5. John Dominic Crossan, *The Dark Interval: Towards a Theology of Story* (Sonoma, Calif.: Polebridge, 1988), 42.

6. Ibid., 66-67.

7. I have found the work of Lankton and Lankton, *Stories of Enchantment: Goal-Oriented Metaphors for Adults and Children in Therapy* (New York: Brunner/Mazel, 1989), very helpful in conceptualizing and developing stories to be told in counseling. The metaphoric protocol is a map or procedure that can be used in designing stories to influence the way people view reality. The protocol attempts to deal with beliefs and convictions about affect, attitudes, and behavior that inform what we do.

8. See Henry Mitchell, *The Recovery of Preaching* (New York: Harper and Row, 1977); *Preaching for Black Self-Esteem* (Nashville: Abingdon, 1994); *Celebration in Preaching* (Abingdon, 1990); and Henry Mitchell and Nicolas Lewter, *Soul Theology* (San Francisco: Harper and Row, 1986).

The approach in this book has a great deal of similarity to the works of Henry Mitchell. He emphasizes preaching as storytelling, speaking to the specific needs of people in a holistic way. For him preaching should emphasize the biblical story and take full advantage of the folk traditions out of which many African Americans and others come.

Although Mitchell's work speaks to the needs of people and addresses their need for self-esteem and affirmation, his works assume an intact culture where supportive values and traditions of hope and care are transmitted through faith communities. He emphasizes a worldview that is supportive of a person's aspirations for personhood in the midst of a society riddled with racism and sexism.

He recognizes that people come to worship with intuitive tapes that need to be recorded again or recorded over. However, his writings do not emphasize enough the task of deconstructing the old tapes before constructing the new ones.

Frank A. Thomas builds on Mitchell's understanding of needing to record over negative tapes. See his *They Like to Never Quit Praisin' God: The Role of Celebration in Preaching* (Cleveland: United Church, 1997). Although his book does not relate to preaching and pastoral counseling, it is an excellent example of pastoral preaching. By this I mean he addresses preaching as building a relationship with people for the purposes of introducing gospel reversals into their lives. He attends to the emotional needs of people in preaching and the emotional processes that would lead to people envisaging God at work in the midst of their lives. His concept of reversals is similar to the concept of parabolic action used in this book in that it refers to God acting in unexpected ways.

The major difference between Thomas's work and my work is in focus. My focus is limited to Jesus' own convictions about himself, his relationship to people with shame and living in shame-prone settings, and the implications these have for how we feel about ourselves. Thomas's focus is on the broad concern of the emotional context of preaching. Thomas also deals with a broader range of emotions. My concern is with shame.

9. Andrew P. Morrison, *The Culture of Shame* (New York: Ballantine Books, 1996), 13.

10. Ibid., 86.

11. Ibid., 95.

12. Merle R. Jordan, *Taking on the Gods: The Task of Pastoral Counseling* (Nashville: Abingdon, 1986), 34.

1. BEYOND THE WORLD OF SHAME

1. See John Dominic Crossan, *Jesus: A Revolutionary Biography* (San Francisco: HarperSan Francisco, 1994), 107.

2. Marcus J. Borg, *Jesus: A New Vision* (San Francisco: Harper, 1987), 42.

3. See Joachim Jeremias, *New Testament Theology* (New York: Charles Scribner's Sons, 1971), 94-96.

4. Borg, *A New Vision*, 79.

5. Ibid., 81.

6. Crossan, *Jesus: A Revolutionary Biography*, 25.

7. Ibid., 70.

8. Ted Peters, *Sin: Radical Evil in Soul and Society* (Grand Rapids: Eerdmans, 1994), 11.

9. Stephen A. Mitchell, *Relational Concepts in Psychoanalysis: An Integration* (Cambridge: Harvard University Press, 1988), 282.

10. Edward P. Wimberly, *African American Pastoral Care* (Nashville: Abingdon, 1990).

2. CAN ANYTHING GOOD COME FROM
THIS SIDE OF THE TRACKS?

1. John Dominic Crossan, *Jesus: A Revolutionary Biography* (San Francisco: HarperSanFrancisco, 1994), 24.

2. John P. Meier, *A Marginal Jew: Rethinking the Historical Jesus*, Vol. 1: *Roots of the Problem and the Person* (New York: Doubleday, 1991), 280.

3. Ibid., 281.

4. This section of the chapter will rely on Gershen Kaufman, *The Psychology of Shame: Theory and Treatment of Shame-Based Syndromes* (New York: Springer, 1996), 271-300.

5. Ibid., 58-60.

6. For a discussion of Jesus as prophet, see Marcus Borg, *Jesus A New Vision: Spirit, Culture, and Life of Discipleship* (San Francisco: HarperSanFrancisco, 1987), 156.

7. Michael E. Kerr and Murray Bowen, *Family Evaluation: An Approach Based on Bowen Theory* (New York: W. W. Norton, 1988), 89-111.

8. Anna-Maria Rizzuto, *The Birth of the Living God: A Psychoanalytic Study* (Chicago: University of Chicago Press, 1979), 182-83.

9. Ibid.

10. Meier, *Marginal Jew,* Vol. 1, 177.

11. For the impact of family secrets on personality development, see Vimala Pillari, *Pathways to Family Myths* (New York: Brunner/Mazel, 1986), 18.

12. Edward P. Wimberly, *Recalling Our Own Stories: The Spiritual Renewal of Religious Caregivers* (San Francisco: Jossey-Bass, 1997).

13. John P. Meier, *Marginal Jew: Rethinking the Historical Jesus*, Vol. 2: *Mentor, Message, and Miracles* (New York: Doubleday, 1994), 1039. Meier says that Jesus' family sharing a vision of Jesus' role in reawakening expectations of the restoration of Israel in all of its glory was wrapped up in the name *Jesus,* which is a form of the name *Joshua.*

14. Wimberly, *Recalling Our Own Stories*, 17.

3. PARENTAL REJECTION

1. Delores S. Williams, *Sisters in the Wilderness: The Challenge of Womanist God-Talk* (Maryknoll, N.Y.: Orbis Books, 1993).

2. Leon Wurmser, *The Mask of Shame* (Baltimore: Johns Hopkins University Press, 1981).

3. Claus Westermann, *The Living Psalms* (Grand Rapids, Mich.: Eerdmans, 1984), 174.

4. Ibid., 82.

5. Ibid., 83.

6. Ibid., 87.

7. Donald Capps, *Biblical Approaches to Pastoral Care* (Philadelphia: Westminster, 1981).

8. Westermann, *The Living Psalms*, 91.

9. John Patton, *Is Human Forgiveness Possible?* (Nashville: Abingdon, 1985).

10. Gershen Kaufman, *The Psychology of Shame: Theory and Treatment of Shame-Based Syndromes* (New York: Springer, 1989), 84.

4. SUCH A FAITH I HAVE NOT SEEN

1. John P. Meier, *Marginal Jew: Rethinking the Historical Jesus,* Vol. 2: *Mentor, Message, and Miracles* (New York: Doubleday, 1994), 725.
2. Ibid., 226.
3. This information is gathered from Joseph A. Fitzmyer, *The Gospel According to Luke* (Garden City, N.Y.: Doubleday, 1981), 652; and *Interpreter's Dictionary of the Bible,* vol. 1 (Nashville: Abingdon, 1962), 547-48; and Meier, *Marginal Jew,* Vol. 2, 718-27.
4. Meier, *Marginal Jew Volume 2,* 718.
5. Norman Perrin, *Rediscovering the Teachings of Jesus* (New York: Harper and Row, 1967).
6. Michael Lewis, *Shame: The Exposed Self* (New York: The Free Press, 1995), 68-73.
7. Gershen Kaufman, *The Psychology of Shame: Theory and Treatment of Shame-Based Syndromes* (New York: Springer, 1996), 44, 54.
8. Ibid., 157.
9. Ibid., 158.
10. Ibid., 161.
11. For a discussion of role taking in narrative, see Edward P. Wimberly, *Using Scripture in Pastoral Counseling* (Nashville: Abingdon, 1994), 25.

5. SHAME AND CONFESSION

1. Gershen Kaufman, *The Psychology of Shame: Theory and Treatment of Shame-Based Syndromes* (New York: Springer, 1989), 271-300.
2. *The Interpreters Bible,* vol. 8 (Nashville: Abingdon, 1952), 143-44.
3. See John Dominic Crossan, *Jesus: A Revolutionary Biography* (San Francisco: HarperSanFrancisco: 1994), 68-69.
4. Michael Lewis, *Shame: The Exposed Self* (New York: Free Press, 1995), 131.
5. Ibid., 71-74.
6. Ibid., 132.
7. Ibid., 134-35.
8. Crossan, *Jesus: A Revolutionary Biography,* 70.
9. Ibid.
10. Ibid., 68.
11. Marcus J. Borg, *Jesus: A New Vision* (San Francisco: HarperSanFrancisco, 1987), 133-135.
12. Ibid.
13. Ibid., 134.
14. See John P. Meier, *Marginal Jew: Rethinking the Historical Jesus: Roots of the Problem and the Person* (New York: Doubleday, 1991), 332-47, 370.
15. For an in-depth treatment of the relationship of boundaries and intimacy, see Carrie Doehring, *Taking Care: Monitoring Power Dynamics and Relational Boundaries in Pastoral Care and Counseling* (Nashville: Abingdon, 1995).
16. For a discussion of identification with biblical characters, see the discussion on role taking in Edward P. Wimberly, *Using Scripture in Pastoral Counseling* (Nashville: Abingdon, 1994), 25-27.

6. COME OUT, YOU UNCLEAN SPIRIT

1. John Dominic Crossan, *Jesus: A Revolutionary Biography* (San Francisco: HarperSanFrancisco, 1994), 88-91. See also Crossan, *The Historical Jesus: The Life of a Mediterranean Jewish Peasant* (San Francisco: HarperSanFrancisco, 1991), 313-18.

2. Crossan, *The Historical Jesus*, 317.

3. Ibid.

4. Ibid.

5. Ibid., 318.

6. See John Richards, *But Deliver Us From Evil: An Introduction to the Demonic Dimension of Pastoral Care* (New York: Seabury, 1974), 19-37; M. Scott Peck, *People of the Lie: The Hope for Healing Human Evil* (New York: Simon and Schuster, 1983), 182-211; Daniel Ryder, *Breaking the Circle of Satanic Ritual Abuse: Recognizing and Recovering from Hidden Trauma* (Minneapolis: CompCare, 1992); and Samuel Southard, "Demonology and Mental Illness" (paper, Fuller Theological Seminary, 1985).

7. Richards, *But Deliver Us From Evil*, 27.

8. Ryder, *Breaking the Circle*, 27-31.

9. Samuel Southard, "Demonology and Mental Illness."

10. For a review of the theory of internalizing biblical scenes related to the Gerasene demoniac, see Edward P. Wimberly, *Using Scripture in Pastoral Counseling* (Nashville: Abingdon, 1994), 33-47.

11. Hymn lyrics from Dottie Rambo, "He Looked Beyond My Fault" (HeartWarming Music, 1968), see *Songs of Zion* (Nashville: Abingdon, 1981), 31.

PART 3: SHAME AND THE PARABLES OF JESUS

1. See Bernard Brandon Scott, *Hear Then the Parable: A Commentary on the Parables of Jesus* (Minneapolis: Fortress, 1989), 79-99.

2. Ibid.

7. A PARENT WHO RISKS BEING SHAMED

1. See Don S. Browning, *Religious Thought and Modern Psychologies* (Philadelphia: Fortress, 1987), 224.

2. Bernard Brandon Scott, *Hear Then the Parable: A Commentary on the Parables of Jesus* (Minneapolis: Fortress, 1989), 110-15.

3. Ibid., 111.

4. Ibid., 113.

5. Ibid.

6. Ibid., 114.

7. Bruce J. Malina, *The New Testament World: Insights from Cultural Anthropology* (Louisville: John Knox, 1987), 27.

8. Ibid., 26-27.

9. Ibid., 28.

10. Ibid., 29.

11. Ibid., 35.

12. Ibid., 117.

13. Edward P. Wimberly, *Recalling Our Own Stories: The Spiritual Renewal of Religious Caregivers* (San Francisco: Jossey-Bass, 1997), 6-9.

14. Michael Lewis, *Shame: The Exposed Self* (New York: The Free Press, 1992), 105-110.

8. HOSPITALITY AT A COST

1. Bernard Brandon Scott, *Hear Then the Parable: A Commentary on the Parables of Jesus* (Minneapolis: Fortress, 1989), 163-65.

2. Ibid., 162.

3. Ibid., 164.

4. Ibid., 173.

5. Ibid., 173-74.

6. John Patton, *Is Human Forgiveness Possible? A Pastoral Care Perspective* (Nashville: Abingdon, 1985), 104-11.

7. Scott, *Hear Then the Parable*, 162-63.

INDEX

SCRIPTURE INDEX